TAKE THE
NEXT STEP

SECRETS TO CREATING SUCCESS
AND MANIFESTING YOUR DREAMS

MAI LIEU

BE THAT
BOOKS®
PUBLISHING

Cover & text design by Tania Craan
Cover Photo © Alfonso Cacciola
Author photograph courtesy of Jason Dziver

Library and Archives Canada Cataloguing in Publication

Lieu, Mai, author
Take the next step : secrets to creating success and manifesting
your dreams / Mai Lieu.

Issued in print and electronic formats.
ISBN 978-1-927897-10-2 (pbk.).
ISBN 978-1-927897-11-9 (pdf)

1. Success in business. 2. Entrepreneurship. 3. Lieu, Mai.
I. Title.

HF5386.L44 2014   650.1   C2014-905711-3
C2014-905712-1

Published in Canada by Be That Books® Publishing

ISBN 10: 1-9278971-0-2
ISBN 13: 978-1-9278971-0-2
Printed and bound in Canada

I dedicate this book to my parents, for overcoming all the obstacles and hardships that have allowed me to have the life I now have.

Table of Contents

Outlining the author's journey from hairstylist to millionaire, while incorporating many of the principles that led to her success. Key concepts including: one step leads to the next step, and you do not need experience to be successful.

The importance of asking for support from family, friends, coaches, accountability partners, and investors. Mai discusses positive support, planning, goal setting, the power of networking and social media, mastermind groups and leadership.

Mai's experience with martial arts fighting in China led to her discovery that fear affects performance. Turn things around with focused intention and certainty, positive thinking and visualization of success.

Through the invention and marketing of her own product, Mai faced challenges and problems. Now, she leads you through the steps to finding the right solution every time.

FOREWORD

Mai Lieu's success story within these pages will inspire you and ignite the entrepreneurial spirit within you that will enable you to make your own dreams a reality. As she shares her story, she skillfully weaves the practical advice that reveals the secrets of her success. When she met a successful single mom who profited from an invention, it triggered her own mind to say, "She did it; I can invent too!"

In reflection, she shares, "I had a burning desire to make it become a reality. I was so clear in my mind that it would work, and I had no doubts at all." Her burning desire and tremendous faith in herself echo the very principles of success outlined by Napoleon Hill in *Think and Grow Rich*, the quintessential book on success and personal development. Had I met her one year earlier, I would have featured Mai Lieu in *Think and Grow Rich for Women* as she serves as a great role model for young women seeking entrepreneurial success today.

While her story is similar to other self-made millionaires and billionaires like Oprah Winfrey, John Paul DeJoria, Do Won Chang, and Li Ka-shing… Mai's story is so much more than just a "rags to riches" story. The book is written in such a way that Mai's story unfolds from her first courageous step in chapter 1 of dropping out of college to pursue her true passion, to conceiving of and building an international brand, to her present day journey as an inspirational speaker and author. And along the way, she lays out each step she took, both the successful ones as well as her "learning opportunities," to get to where she is today. As she reveals her personal struggles and triumphs you will share her journey and after you have finished reading *Take the Next Step*, you will feel that you know Mai as a personal friend.

She will inspire you to take action using her 23 exercises, sprinkled throughout the book, designed to build your entrepreneurial muscles as well as your mental strength through their personal development benefits as well. As Mai writes, "For business, I think it's just as important to continue investing in your personal development as it is to continue planning and setting goals. It's like the gym; you can buy the membership, but if you don't go and lift those weights, you won't get those muscles. Also, if you stop using them, your muscles disappear."

Take the Next Step is written in a light, conversational style, with humor and heart, as if Mai were your personal business and life coach. Within these pages she shares a roadmap for you to chart your own course for spiritual and material success. I invite you to take the first step.

To your success!

Sharon Lechter, CPA CGMA
Author of *Think and Grow Rich for Women*
Co-author of *Outwitting the Devil, Three Feet From Gold,* and *Rich Dad Poor Dad*
and 14 other books in the *Rich Dad* series.

INTRODUCTION

I am a self-made millionaire. I have created success and I am living the life of my dreams. In this book, I reveal the secrets of creating success so that you too can make millions! Just a few years ago, I was a full-time hairstylist, and I was tired of standing for ten hours a day. My back hurt, and I had tendonitis in my hand. I needed to figure out a way to MAKE MONEY WHILE I SLEPT! I had many opportunities to start my own salon; however, from what I saw, owning my own salon seemed like it would take up MORE of my time.

I desired to create freedom, not just financially, but all around. I desired to be able to surf all day (if I fancied to). I desired to make a difference on a bigger level. I desired to feel passion again, and most of all, I desired to create PASSIVE INCOME!

But the first thing I had to do was to declare to myself what it was that I desired, and to be open for guidance from the universe. Only one week after I put it out to the universe, the idea and vision came to me. I knew this was it! I had a burning desire to make it become a reality. It was so clear in my mind that it would work, and I had no doubts at all.

I felt like I was on fire; when people around me tried to put down my idea, it just bounced right off me and gave me the fuel to go even further.

I was off to follow this big and exciting dream! But I knew I had to work smarter, not harder. And that's just what I created. I love waking up in the morning and checking how many orders I received overnight. It is always so exciting to see the orders coming in from all over the world. I'm just an ordinary woman who had no experience inventing, yet I did it. If I can do it, you can too!

EXERCISE:
FINDING YOUR HEART'S DESIRE

Sit on a cushion; close your eyes. Slow your breathing and focus on each inhalation and exhalation. Take a breath in and slowly release. With each release, count in your head, and continue with each inhalation and exhalation, counting all the way to ten. Once you feel centered, ask yourself, "What is it that I would do for free? What is it that I just love doing and time just flies when I'm doing it?" Wait for the answer and just be open to what might arise. If it doesn't come right away, it's okay. Go about your day and remember to ask the same questions in your mind. When the time is right, the insight will drop in when you least expect it. Remember, life's guidance comes when you are present and grounded.

CHAPTER 1

WHAT IS YOUR DREAM?
TAKE THE NEXT STEP

---

*Don't wait until everything is just right. It will never be perfect.
There will always be challenges, obstacles and less than perfect
conditions. So what. Get started now. With each step you take,
you will grow stronger and stronger, more and more skilled, more
and more self-confident and more and more successful.*
—*Mark Victor Hansen*

I desire to share with you all of the things that have helped me along the way. I am sharing my secret with you because I believe that...

TOGETHER WE CAN CREATE MORE.

I am very grateful to be living the life of my dreams, and each day I have more things to be grateful for. I never would have thought my life would transform from being a hairstylist to a full-time Inventor and business owner all because I explored an opportunity and took a risk. I know this is just the beginning. I have a very big vision and I know I have lots to contribute!

Are you ready to create more opportunity in your life?

Here are four simple steps to get you moving:

1. Start asking for what you desire. When you ask, things start to happen. You start to think creatively. You start to see the opportunities around you.
2. Wait for guidance from the universe. Be open to what life brings to you. Explore possibilities!
3. Listen to your intuition; it will always guide you in the right direction.
4. Take the risk; without risk, nothing will change!

For two solid years, I was so clear and on purpose; I felt like I was climbing a mountain! I would take one step and then the next step, not hesitating but, instead, just trusting myself and committing, not looking back. I was open, flexible, trusting, willing, risking, vulnerable, capable, excited, determined, and solution oriented. Whatever I needed to bring to the table, I brought that out in me. I flowed like water effortlessly because I didn't resist anything. I just used the momentum and rode the waves of the universe.

In less than two years, my dreams have become a reality. In front of millions, live on the Home Shopping Network (HSN), the spokesperson confirmed that I had sold out of CreaClips in 13 minutes flat! It was a dream come true. I had done it! I had envisioned a day where I would invent a product, develop it, manufacture it, and sell it on TV. I realized that everything that had happened in my life up to that point had influenced me in becoming a successful entrepreneur.

Have you ever been stuck in a career, a job, or a place where you know you are doing something that is NOT WHAT YOU DESIRE, but you are too afraid to take a risk?

In my third year at the University of Calgary, I realized that Accounting was not what I desired to do with the rest of my life. I had always loved playing with hair; I would style my friends' hair at school and at ten years old, I even began cutting my friends' hair. But as I was finishing school, everyone (especially my parents) thought the right thing to do was to get a degree. It was what everyone did, after all.

My parents wanted me to be a doctor or a lawyer; accounting was my compromise. I didn't know until after I got into it, how much I didn't like it, and it was the opposite of what I really desired to do. It got so bad that I had to force myself to go to my class each day. My intuition was screaming, THIS IS NOT IT! But I didn't know what else to do.

AT LEAST I KNEW ONE THING—I LEARNED WHAT I DIDN'T LIKE AND IT LED ME CLOSER TO WHAT I DID LIKE!

One day, my boyfriend at the time was asked to be a model for a photo shoot. I was kind of jealous, so I went along with him. What I did not know? That day would be the start of my transformation. I got to see Hung Vanngo do his magic. He was doing hair and makeup for the models at his own photo shoot for a hair magazine competition. I knew right then and there that THIS was what I desired to be doing. I was so inspired that I told my boyfriend, "This is where I was heading and what I desired to do career-wise." Surprisingly, he was very supportive and said, "Just go for it."

WHEN YOU ARE INSPIRED, LISTEN TO YOUR INTUITION AND TAKE ACTION!

I went home and told my mom that I desired to drop out of university and enroll in hair school. It didn't go well, to say the least. She said, "You only have one year left; just finish it." Back then, hairstylists didn't make much money, and, to her, that wasn't a very prestigious job. My mom was very upset and gave me the two knuckles to my head. I knew I was in deep trouble when I got that! It seemed like an Asian thing that parents did as punishment. I was not only afraid to disappoint my mom, but I was also afraid to fail. I was grateful that somewhere along the way, I learned that...

IF YOU DESIRE TO GROW, YOU HAVE TO TAKE RISKS!

My parents always said that as I was growing up. They had many businesses and they took risks. They also became successful. Now when I look back,

FEAR SHOWED ME I WAS HEADING IN THE RIGHT DIRECTION!

When I was young, we were very poor. We came to Canada when I was 4 years old, and we had nothing. My mom worked at McDonald's and my Dad worked two jobs, even night shifts. I didn't have toys or dolls growing up, so I tied a bunch of string together and pretended it was hair. I braided it, and it would entertain me for hours. I had found something I was passionate about, hair.

WHAT IS IT THAT YOU ARE PASSIONATE ABOUT AND WHAT INSPIRES YOU?

What is it that you can't stop thinking about? What is it that you would do—even for free? I believe as long as you follow your passion, you will always be successful. You are more willing to overcome obstacles because it's what you love to do. No one has to force you to get out of bed to do what you love. When I'm doing what I love, it doesn't feel like work, time flies and I could do it for hours. Confucius said, "CHOOSE A JOB YOU LOVE, AND YOU WILL NEVER HAVE TO WORK A DAY IN YOUR LIFE."

Dropping out of university was a very big risk; however, after taking that next step and going into hair school, I realized that it took more energy to hold back than to just go for it! I remembered how hard it was each day—I didn't know how much longer I could do it. I was drained every day, fighting the urge to quit, forcing myself to do what I did not desire. But, once I got in to hair school, I had so much energy! I was alive again. I was so inspired to learn, and I desired to absorb everything.

JUST TAKE ONE STEP, ANY STEP, AND IT WILL LEAD YOU TO THE NEXT. IT IS BETTER TO TAKE ANY STEP, THAN TO NEVER TAKE A STEP AT ALL.

Sometimes, by doing so many things wrong, it narrows your choices down to what you DO like. There is nothing worse than looking back, regretting, and saying, "I should have."

During hair school, my teacher thought I was very talented and suggested that I enter the "Young Protégé Hair" competition. She believed I would have a good chance of winning. I've had teachers in the past who told me I was not smart at certain subjects, and their words affected my grades. But I chose not to listen to those teachers. I chose to listen to the ones who gave positive feedback. Positive feedback encouraged me to do better! Positive words were planted in my head, and that's what I created, that's what I chose to believe. In fifth grade, my math teacher, Mr. Martin, told me I was brilliant and that I was a genius and would go far in life. I don't know if this was exactly true back then, but I believed it, and it helped me build my confidence as a young child and later as an adult. What you believe becomes your truth.

IT'S WHAT YOU CREATE IN YOUR MIND THAT CAN INFLUENCE YOUR LIFE. FOCUS ON THE POSITIVE THOUGHTS!

Trusting my cosmetology teacher's kind words, I entered the hair competition and won first place for all of Alberta. The prize was a trip to Toronto to compete against the rest of Canada's best!

I remember how excited I was to embark on my first trip outside of Alberta. I loved every moment of it, and the experience really opened me up to what was possible outside of Calgary. And you know what? I won SECOND place! I started to think, "Wow! Maybe I can be good at this, maybe I can be a successful hairstylist."

WHEN YOU GET MOMENTUM, KEEP MOVING FORWARD!

THE UNIVERSE ONLY GIVES YOU OPPORTUNITIES YOU ARE READY FOR, BUT IF YOU DON'T TAKE IT, IT MOVES ON TO THE NEXT PERSON

My motto is: "Just go for it!" The worst that could happen is that it might lead you to something else. You learn from every experience, so you can never fail! Failure does not exist if you always learn from the experience. I look at everything in life as a learning opportunity, and I trust it will lead me to something great.

Once I got my Cosmetology license, I entered the ABA (Alberta Beauty Association) Professional Hair Competition. The competition was full of professional stylists, with over twenty years of hair experience and this time, it was not for students. This time, it was for professionals only! The largest trade show in Alberta, with thousands of people in attendance and I'm on stage with only thirty minutes to create a cutting-edge hairstyle. When the timer went off, I was in the zone. I didn't even pay attention to the thousands of people watching me. I was so focused and present!

WHEN YOU ARE DOING WHAT YOU LOVE, YOU ARE IN THE ZONE.

I could hear my intuition saying, "This is great, you are on the right track," and at the end, I had created an amazing haircut that won first place. I couldn't believe it! I had won first place against hairstylists with twenty years experience. That was my first lesson:

YOU DO NOT HAVE TO HAVE EXPERIENCE TO BE SUCCESSFUL!

Straight out of hair school and I won! It was so exciting, and my parents were so proud of me. They had been concerned when I quit university and likely thought I wasn't serious, but they came around and saw how much I loved doing hair, and that I was actually good!

I started asking myself better questions, like "What else am I passionate about?" At that time, I loved doing martial arts. My father had always loved demonstrating kung fu to our family. I thought it was so cool, but it wasn't until I was nineteen before I actually took my first class. My teacher, Alex Kwok, who is world renowned, had won many competitions back in the 60s and 70s. He was on the cover of martial arts magazines everywhere. He was even asked to play Bruce Lee's role after he had passed away during filming. Alex not only taught me kung fu, but he opened me up to so many new experiences and taught me how to focus and practice self-discipline.

The first day of training, one of Alex's students, Vince, was teaching me the "block punch" move. Alex would come around and check my movements. It was a basic move; you use your left hand and block upward and then punch with your strong right hand!

I was only one week into training when he said, "Okay, you are ready. There's a competition next week that I'd like you to enter!" I was shocked and scared! Confused, I asked, "What? It's only been one week and I only know one move." Vince said, "Okay, I'll teach you a side kick; okay kick! Now you know two moves! You are ready!" I surrendered and trusted him. I remembered that.

THE UNIVERSE ONLY GIVES
YOU OPPORTUNITIES YOU ARE READY FOR.

That weekend, when we were at the competition, my opponent came charging at me (out of control) and so, I reacted with the block punch and, surprisingly, I got a point! She came charging recklessly again, and I did it again! It was hilarious that I got so many points from just that one move. It was simple and effective, and since I had focused all my efforts practicing, it felt like a natural reflex. I won first place and the trophy they gave me was almost as tall as me!

YOU CAN BE SUCCESSFUL,
EVEN IF YOU DON'T KNOW HOW TO DO IT!

I can look back and see that martial arts was actually preparing me. I went on to compete in many competitions, winning all of the ones in Canada before heading into the United States. When I first started, I was competing in point fighting. But, after winning all of the competitions, I had moved up to full contact fighting. It was more of a challenge and I always like to GROW AND TAKE IT TO THE NEXT LEVEL.

Full Contact Fighting is called Sanda or Sanshou, literally meaning, "free fighting." It combines kickboxing and takedowns, throws and sweeps. You fight on a platform and you also get points if you run the opponent off the platform.

At this time in my life, I continued doing hair competitions and won seven first-place international beauty awards. I traveled to the USA to the biggest hair shows and trained with the top academies.

SUCCESSFUL PEOPLE CONTINUE TO LEARN
AND BECOME EXPERTS IN THEIR FIELD.

So... what was the next step? That's something I always do; I always ask myself, "What is the next step?" That way, I never stop progressing and I never stop growing. The next step would be my biggest step yet. I thought, "Why not go live in China and learn from the experts!?"

IF YOU DESIRE TO BE THE BEST, GO LEARN FROM THE BEST!

In Beijing China, training with professionals at the sports university, I got to meet Jet Li's teacher. I was also able to see a professional Wushu team train. The highlight each weekend was a live show where the competitors came to fight. That meant that each weekend, I got to watch the best in China compete.

When I look back, I am really grateful to have experienced China back then, as many things have changed over the years and there were many things I got to do then that they don't allow now. It was the most exciting time of my life. The city grew fast and I got to experience old traditional China.

TAKE THE NEXT STEP, TAKE THE RISK AND GO FOR IT!

When I first went to China, it was only supposed to be for three months; however, I loved it so much that I kept calling my dad and telling him that I was going to stay a little longer. I kept extending it for three month intervals, and I ended up staying for two years!

SOMETIMES YOU JUST HAVE TO TAKE AN UNCERTAIN STEP
SO YOU WILL KNOW IF IT IS TRULY WHAT YOU DESIRE.

I wasn't sure if I would like living in China, so I thought three months would be sufficient. But I was having so much fun in a new country with many new things to experience. Plus, I got to do what I loved! Extending my stay in China meant I needed a way to make money to pay for my expenses. I had only saved up enough money to cover my first three months. Why not combine my two passions?

I landed a job doing hair for expatriates from various countries while still training in martial arts. I worked at a high-end salon, I had a great boss, and, on top of it all, he was from Australia. I learned a lot styling international clients! The local Chinese had very little experience in hair styling and were not trained in cutting foreign hair. They would get nervous at the sight of curly hair and would mess up trying to do the same techniques they would do for Asian hair. They always thinned it out too much. I ended up fixing a lot of haircuts that the locals had done. My skills were very much needed, plus being able to speak English was a bonus. My Chinese was getting really good too. What I did not know then was that this was an important step in my journey as an inventor!

WHEN YOU LEARN FROM THE EXPERTS IN YOUR FIELD, YOU BECOME AN EXPERT.

So I did my research. Canada was part of the Commonwealth and if I was under twenty-eight years of age, I could get a working holiday Visa for Europe and Australia easily. This visa allowed me to work and travel all over Europe for up to two years, so I jumped at the chance and took my next step! I was able to participate in some photo shoots while I was there, and I loved doing hair and fashion shows. My favorite experience was attending Vidal Sassoon's hair academy and the Toni and Guy Academy! They were the leading educators at the time. I always learn from the best. Bonus for me; I got to backpack around Europe!

One of the secrets to my success is that I always continue to learn and grow. When you specialize in something, you are irreplaceable and in higher demand! That's how I earned the right to do celebrities hair and later specialize in hair extensions.

After Europe, I asked myself, "Where else would I love to live?" When I was a little girl, I would have dreams about living in Hawaii with beautiful tropical fruit trees. I was very much into snowboarding at Lake Louise, but had a burning desire to learn how to surf. I thought that I could always go there for a year and if I didn't like it, I could go back. Another important lesson:

IF IT DOESN'T WORK OUT, YOU CAN ALWAYS GO BACK.

My first day in Hawaii, I learned how to surf, and I was hooked. I had found a new passion, even though it meant getting up at 6 a.m! For seven years straight, I surfed almost every day. I would surf for two hours and then go to work. I got a job at Paul Brown, one of the top hair salons in Hawaii. My boss and manager were great; so supportive and very caring.

Riding the waves in Hawaii!

Paul Brown was an inspiration to me. He was very famous and had his own product line. "Dog, the bounty hunter" was a frequent client, and he asked me to do his hair! I also did Don Ho's hair before he passed away. He was one of the most famous celebrities in Hawaii, and I was probably the only person who didn't know who he was. I was in his dressing room and saw a photo of him shaking Elvis's hand, and it hit me *"Maybe Don Ho is famous?"* I did his hair, not even knowing who he was. He was so pleasant, and he sang "Tiny Bubbles" the whole time I did his hair. He liked that I didn't know who he was at first, and I was grateful for another amazing experience I would never forget.

I WAS THANKFUL FOR ATTRACTING THESE AMAZING OPPORTUNITIES.

Three years zoomed by fast and I had reached a point where I wasn't growing anymore. Logically, the next step would be to open my own salon, but I didn't see any freedom in that. I desired to have the freedom to be able to work only if I felt like it and to surf all day if I chose.

I DESIRED TO MAKE MONEY WHILE I SLEPT.

I loved doing hair, but I didn't like standing on my feet ten hours a day; my back hurt and I had tendonitis in my wrist and thumb. It really sucked when the doctors told me I had to stop doing hair. With tears, I said, "Anna, this is what I love. What do you mean I have to stop?" I knew that I would have to find a new passion.

It wasn't until I took a personal and professional growth seminar called PSI (Personal Success Institute, www.psiseminars.com) that I really began to understand what I had to do next. People called this seminar a "dream vehicle." It taught them how to break through their fears and help them get to their dreams faster! I had already created so much success, but I thought that it could only help me create more success.

PSI was the beginning of my spiritual growth journey. It was what I was looking for. When I was competing in martial arts, I always felt that I wanted to manage my thoughts and fears better. I learned so many tools in this seminar to direct my attention and to think positive. This was it!

I was so inspired that weekend. I realized that even though I enjoyed working at the salon, I had reached a point where I was not growing anymore and I desired to create financial liberty.

WHEN THINGS GET TOO COMFORTABLE, IT IS A SIGN YOU ARE NOT GROWING ANY MORE.

I set a ninety-day goal to patent my invention and move forward and went home to be with my family in Canada. It was only one week after the seminar when the idea came to me. I was with my brother at one of his meetings in a restaurant, and I was bored and daydreaming. When I saw a waitress walking by, I noticed that she had long hair, and the idea dropped in from the universe. Actually, it was more than just the idea; it was a vision of how my idea would benefit millions of people and allow me to realize my dream of financial liberty.

In my experience, everything starts with a vision. I believe that when you can see it in your mind, you can make it a reality. However, it is important that the moment you have an inspired thought, YOU HAVE TO TAKE IMMEDIATE ACTION! I found that, oftentimes, if I didn't take immediate action, the negative voice in my head would start to talk me out of it. That's why I never wait very long to do something I'm inspired to do.

I had a feeling that this was it; this was what I had been asking for.

I decided two things:
1. I was going to take the next step in my dreams, no matter what.
2. I made a commitment to my personal growth, to continue to expand my way of thinking. I knew from past experience that fear affected my performance. I desired to empower myself so nothing could get in my way!

I was so excited, I told my brother about the idea right away. He said, "Don't tell anyone just yet... not even Mom." We had over 500 family members in Calgary, so news like this could spread fast! When I desire something, I make a commitment. I usually tell people what I am going to do, and I put it out to the universe. I find that if I keep the idea inside, I tend to talk myself out of it. By telling others about my goal, it keeps me accountable. I started telling people my goal, but I wouldn't tell them what my invention was. I wanted to patent it first, just to be on the safe side. I realize now, I should have listened to my brother's advice. If you tell people your goal too soon, their negative thinking may discourage you and talk you out of going for it. As with some great lessons, I learned this one the hard way.

When I returned home to Hawaii, I was on fire! I began to research online the "how-to" steps of creating an invention. I also went to the bookstore and got all the books I could find about inventing. The first step was to make a prototype. I went to a hardware store and to the craft store for starter supplies. It helped to walk up and down the aisle to see what they had and gain some ideas for materials to use.

I used papier-mâché and chicken wire to create my first prototype

With papier-mâché and chicken wire, I started building. I had a pile of newspaper, and I had even ripped out positive words and pasted them onto my prototype. For several hours straight, I was in the zone. When I finished, it was 1:00 in the morning, and I had a shield with VelcroTM straps. It really didn't matter what it looked like; I just needed to test the functionality. I could tweak and change it later.

SOMETIMES, IT IS ENOUGH TO TAKE A STEP, ANY STEP, AND IT WILL LEAD YOU TO THE NEXT.

The creation step was the most enjoyable and exciting part of inventing! I had no idea what I was doing... I just started to create.

The first step in the invention process is to create a working prototype, it doesn't matter what it looks like.

The next day, after the papier-mâché prototype had dried, I thought, "Okay, I have to test this." I called my friend Kaoru, who had long hair, and she informed me that she had not cut her hair for two years! She would be a perfect model! She was such a good sport too, and she told me to do whatever I thought best. Hairstylists love to hear that!

The first cut with my prototype!

I turned Kaoru around and strapped the prototype shield on her back. I fastened each strap of VelcroTM around her shoulder to keep it in place. Kaoru had a confused, scared look on her face and asked, "What's going on? I thought you were going to cut my hair?" I said, "Yes we are. Don't worry; just let me test this..." and quickly, I turned her around.

SOMETIMES YOU HAVE TO FAKE IT TILL YOU MAKE IT.

Once the prototype was in place, I cut a perfect straight-across cut in less than sixty seconds. It actually worked! I had that gut feeling and knew that I had to develop this product. My intuition was screaming, "GO FOR IT!"

I called my brother and my parents to tell them my idea actually worked. I still hadn't told them exactly what it was, but they were happy for me and encouraged me to continue.

While the first prototype worked just great, there were still a few improvements needed. The shield was a little too big to use and store, so people would not likely buy it like this. I started to brainstorm on how I could make it smaller. And then, just like Einstein, Thomas Edison, Elias Howe, and other famous scientists and inventors, I found myself waking up in the middle of the night with solutions.

MAKE SURE YOU WRITE DOWN
ALL OF YOUR IDEAS WHEN YOU HAVE THEM.

It is so easy to forget ideas that pop into your head, especially in the middle of the night when you wake up from a dream. I decided to keep a notebook by my bed and write ideas down, even if it was 3 a.m. I also kept an inventors journal. I found that I had a lot of ideas during the night, so don't stress out if that happens to you. Force yourself to write down ONLY the raw idea and try not to analyze it and refine it. Then go back to sleep. I often wake up with an inspired thought during the night, which leads to productive work during the day!

WHEN YOU ASK FOR WHAT YOU DESIRE,
THE UNIVERSE WILL FIND A WAY TO GET IT TO YOU.

You have to be in a centered space to receive good ideas. If I am angry with someone or have resentment, it is hard to be inspired or to think of solutions. It's important to clear anything that takes up space in your mind or drains your energy. It was 3 a.m. when I woke up with an idea of how to make my invention smaller. All of a sudden, I thought, "I don't require the whole shield; I can actually cut off half of the parts, since they're not in use anymore." I ended up turning the shield into a clip.

I went back to hardware and craft stores in search of materials for the second prototype I had envisioned. I have always been a creative person and I love arts and crafts. Inventing was just another way I could express my creativity.

YOU DON'T KNOW WHAT THE NEXT STEP IS...
UNTIL YOU TAKE THE FIRST STEP.

After making my first prototype, I knew that the next prototype had to be smaller. This is why I always tell people:

"JUST TAKE A STEP AND IT WILL LEAD YOU TO THE NEXT STEP."

I knew exactly what needed to be done next, and I made at least five prototypes before I arrived at the final design.

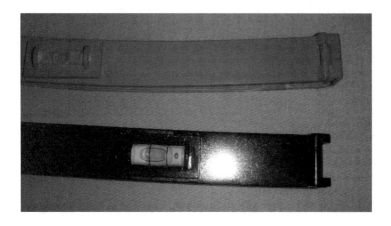

Early prototypes of the CreaClip that didn't make the cut!

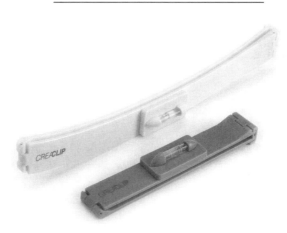

The final CreaClip Products!

The CreaClip in action!

Fortunately, I had made some very supportive friends in Hawaii, so I decided to form a focus group to get feedback on my product. I made sure I asked positive friends. This is a key factor in taking the next step toward creating success, which I will be discussing in more detail in chapter 2. My friend Tina was always very positive and I knew she would always say supportive things. That's what I needed to hear because it gave me confidence!

EXERCISE:

WHAT'S YOUR NEXT STEP?

Visualize yourself doing what you love. You may not see how you can get from your present situation to doing what you love. But don't worry about that. Lao Tzu said, "A journey of a thousand miles begins with a single step." So focus on that one step. What is it you can do right now that will help you reach your goal? Maybe it's something as safe and simple as researching it on the Internet. Now, go for it.

Tahitian dancing is another passion for me. Always do what you love!

TAKE A STEP, ANY STEP. IT'S BETTER THAN NO STEP AT ALL!

Just take a step toward your dreams; any step is better than no step at all. When you take one step, it will lead you to the next. Even if it's not the right step, you will learn something that will take you even closer to your goal. Thomas Edison made hundreds of wrong steps in the process of inventing the light bulb, but each wrong step led him to the next innovation and the next step closer, till finally, his idea lit up the world. There are so many people stuck because they don't know what to do next, or they don't have all the right answers, or they want everything perfect before they take action. For me, I just take one step that my heart wants, letting go of any expectations about it being a certain way. That way, I just do what is required in the present moment. Then, once I'm done with that, I take the next step. It's much easier this way and I don't get overwhelmed. When I look back and see all that I have done with my business, if I had known when I first started what I would have to go through, I'm sure I would have been discouraged. When you're driving a car in the middle of the night, you can only see as far as the lights shine. That's all you require to get to your destination. Take the first step. Once you do that, it will lead you to the next step.

I had the mindset of no expectations, so it really helped me to be more receptive and creative. Sometimes, not knowing what you're do-ing has its advantages. I had no experience inventing, so I also didn't have any expectations. I just did what I thought seemed best at the time. People would ask me, "How much do you sell your product for?" Some people were surprised that I was able to sell my product for such a high price. If I had known that the industry standard wholesale price for my type of product was eight dollars, I would have priced my prod-uct there. But because I didn't know, I priced the CreaClip at twelve dollars, which I thought was fair, and it was what I desired. The same can apply when it comes to your salary. People sometimes don't ask for what they feel is fair because it's higher than the standard salary range, but I'm saying break that standard; be the one who gets paid for what you're worth! You can always ask, and the worst thing that can happen is they say no, but, if you don't ask, you won't even have the opportunity!

The advantage of not knowing how to do something is that you can create your own path. Personally, I don't follow the standard; I just do it the way I desire to. I don't follow what's been done. Leaders create their own path. I hosted an event in Canada recently, and rather than hosting it in a standard hotel ballroom, I held the event at a cozy, relaxing lounge. It was so much fun and out of the box. I just created my own path instead of following the beaten path. There are so many paths to create, just make one of your own. Sometimes it's better not to know exactly what you are doing, because knowing only one way might influence you the wrong way! Be careful with your own expectations; if you don't meet them, you might think things are not happening the right way. When people say, "But I don't know how," I say, "Great! That will be to your advantage!" Many famous inventors including Steve Jobs, Frank Lloyd Wright, George Eastman, Henry Ford, Thomas Edison, and Walt Disney, dropped out of high school or college and never learned the "right way" to do something; they created a better way.

When I made my first prototype, I simply created what I could see in my mind. After I made the first one, I was able to see ways of improving it, and that led to the next prototype, and then the next. See? If I hadn't taken one step, I wouldn't have known which direction to go. Also, if I hadn't taken the step of going to cosmetology school, I may not have become an inventor. If I had not become an inventor, I may not have become a bestselling author or inspirational speaker! EVERYTHING LEADS TO THE NEXT THING. I did not know when I took the first step of going to cosmetology school that my life would follow this path, and I'm glad I didn't know. WHATEVER THE IDEA, JUST TAKE A STEP!

ASK AND YOU SHALL RECEIVE!

I can't believe how many times this happens to me. I put my desires out to the Universe, and they come. When I needed a packaging designer for my product, I got a call from my cousin who does packaging the same day I was thinking I needed it! One day, a friend and I were talking about how nice it would be to own a hot tub. I had wanted one for a while, but I hadn't purchased one because they were just too expensive. Not long after this conversation, that same friend messaged me to ask if I was interested in a free hot tub. A friend was getting rid of theirs and all I had to do was pay to have it shipped! I was shocked and impressed at how fast the universe worked.

I wanted to move to the Big Island, and while I had never been there, I had heard that it was amazing. Our first trip was a house hunting mission. We looked at a few houses, found our perfect dream home, and, the next day, made an offer. We felt blessed that our dream house was waiting for us to see that day; the owner had been ready to take it off the market and rent it out for a year! Everything was in alignment for us to see it, and the next day, we made an offer. We were so clear it was the perfect house for us, and we love it! It sounds really risky to some people that, out of the blue, we decided to buy a house on the Big Island, but it felt right to us.

I always practice saying my desires and goals out loud, and I make sure I tell people. This keeps me accountable, and if people can help me somehow, they will! You never know; someone may know of someone who can connect you to what you desire. But make sure you tell only positive, supportive people. When you ask for something, you are ready to receive it!

EXERCISE:
ASK THE UNIVERSE

Start now and ask for what you desire, and say it out loud to the universe. Be sure you frame your desire using positive words. Instead of saying "need" or "want," which have the connotation of lack, say "require" or "desire." And, instead of a request or demand, frame it as a thank you in advance. Say, "I am grateful to the universe for fulfilling my desire for <insert what you desire to have>!"

CHAPTER 2

ASK FOR SUPPORT

Needing help doesn't make you weak, in fact quite the opposite.
It makes you strong, smart, resourceful, and realistic. Being prideful
is a weakness. Asking for help when you know you're in
over your head is strength. Don't ever forget that!
—*Stephenie Zamora*

I reached a point with my business where I was stuck. I knew something was holding me back from taking it to the next level. But what? I had always heard from various success seminars, that "together you can create more." However, I was stubborn and independent, and told myself, "You don't need help; you can do it yourself. Don't ask for support because you don't want to bother them." I had lived my life doing everything myself, never once asking for support. Why start now?

Well, what I have learned is that when I ask for and accept support, I can be much more effective! Plus, It's more enjoyable, and others will feel good about their contributions. I have always given support and helped others, but I felt bad asking others to help me. This was very unbalanced.

WHEN YOU DON'T ALLOW OTHERS TO SUPPORT YOU,
YOU ARE ACTUALLY TAKING FROM THEM.

I was all for helping them, but I would never let them return the favor. Someone once told me, "Mai, you are always helping others and you don't allow others to help you; you are actually taking because you deprive them of the satisfaction of helping you." I didn't think of it that way. When I help people, I feel really good inside, but if I don't allow others to do the same for me, I'm not allowing them to feel good. So I started to ask for support.

When it was time for me to file for a patent for my invention, I made an appointment with a local patent attorney. I was afraid; I had so many negative voices. "You're just this little girl; what do you know about patents?" The voice in my head was correct; I was just a hairstylist and I didn't know a thing about inventing. I realized I needed help before meeting with the patent attorney.

So I decided to call Sam King, an acquaintance I had recently made, who was also an attorney. It was hard for me to ask because I had just met him a few weeks before. I asked him, "Sam, what goes on in a meeting with a patent attorney?" I admitted to Sam that I felt like a little girl with no experience. Sam said, "Well, if I don't have court, I'll go with you." I was shocked. I couldn't believe that he would do that for me. Instantly, I felt relieved.

Unfortunately, Sam did have to go to court that day, but he asked his wife, Adrienne, who also was an attorney, to go with me instead. Sitting in the meeting, I felt confident and a little bit like a 'hot shot' because I had my own attorney with me, while discussing patents for my invention. Adrienne had a great time at the meeting, too; she learned a lot. I thought it was bad to ask for help, but I realized that it was okay if both parties involved benefitted from it. It was a fair exchange and a win–win situation! I also decided to start hanging around like-minded people. People who thought positively, who were growing, and who were interested in personal growth—other entrepreneurial types. This allowed me to ask for support and to give support without feeling guilty.

SURROUND YOURSELF WITH POSITIVE SUPPORT.

I was very good in math, and all that problem solving in school really paid off. I was so fortunate to have a great math teacher, Mr. Martin.

He always told me in front of the class, "Mai, you have a great brain; you are so smart, brilliant." I didn't think I was, but because he said it, I started to believe it. He thought I'd be a great math teacher. What a nice compliment! I started to take math serious and became very good at it. I have to thank him for being such a great teacher and influence in my life.

If you have people around you who say positive words to you, even if you don't initially believe it, you will start to believe it! It can also work the opposite way; negative words can influence you too. That's why I surround myself with positive-thinking people who support me in my vision!

I found it hard to go after my dreams surrounded by negative people who were always more interested in dragging me down rather than lifting me up. My older brother made a good point one day when he said that it's a lot harder to try to quit smoking when everyone around you smokes! If people around me kept telling me that my invention sucked, there was a very good chance that I might start to believe it.

There were enough negative voices in my own head that I had to deal with, and I did not need my environment to be filled with external negative thoughts and words. Be protective of your environment—if people are negative, they can really drag you down and influence your way of thinking. When people say that I'm stupid or that my idea is stupid, I likely already have that negative self-doubt ruminating around in my head. So when someone else says it, my doubts are confirmed and it makes the negativity more believable. Choose carefully who you desire to be in your space and in your circle of friends. Motivational speaker Jim Rohn said, "You are the average of the five people you spend the most time with." I would add "including yourself," and it is a powerful truth that our environments do influence us. Choose friends who see you, your qualities, and your potential as more than you see of yourself; friends who are there to support you.

One of my coworkers laughed at me when I told him my idea. It was very discouraging. Another coworker said, "You really don't think you are going to invent something and make money, do you?" The negativity was hard to deal with, so I was grateful that I had made some great friends through the PSI seminars. My new circle of friends were into entrepreneurship, thinking positively, and were interested in grow-ing. They were great cheerleaders!

The network of friends that I had created became my support sys-tem. When I was feeling doubtful during difficult times and I felt like I couldn't do it or when I wanted to give up, I would call up a friend, and he or she would lift me up. When I found out it was going to cost me $200,000 to invent, develop, and market the CreaClip, I was left wondering how the heck I was ever going to do it. I imagined the de-velopment costs to be around $50,000, but $200,000!? That was crazy! A supportive friend told me, "Mai, the universe gave you this idea and if you don't do it, you're not going to have more inventions!"

"Wow! That's so true!" I thought. All I needed to hear was that I could do it, and it empowered me to just keep moving forward... to keep taking that next step. Be sure to have at least one person you can count on who you know will support you. There will be times when you feel like giving up, and you can always just call them to lift you up!

It wasn't until I decided to patent my invention that things really got rolling. At first, I did some procrastinating, but I knew I had to set a goal and commit. Putting money towards a patent meant I HAD to be committed because a patent can cost between $5,000 and $25,000. If I was really going to do this, I had to be prepared to follow through.

The first investors in my company were my family. Investors are more willing to invest if they also believe in you and NOT just your idea. Investors desire to know that you will follow through and that you are committed. The people who know you best are more willing to invest in you. My family didn't even know what my invention was because I wanted to keep it a secret until it was patent pending, yet they still invested in my company. I was so grateful to have such a trusting and supportive family. Plus, I knew I was going to make millions with this invention, so I desired to share it with the people I loved most.

At first, I opened it up to family investors and then to close friends. Once I had created success, lots of investors approached me and I had to turn them away. When I was open to taking on more investors, their capital allowed me to grow even faster. It's easy to get investors when you have proven you are committed to your dream, and you can prove that you are working your business plan.

Once the patent was processed, things started coming together. The hardest part of the inventing process for me was all the back and forth thinking and debating—should I do it, or should I not? I took a year to think about it before filing the patent but, as soon as I had committed to it, there was momentum.

ACCOUNTABILITY PARTNER/COACHES!

I find it very beneficial to have a coach. In sports, we have coaches to push us further than we think we can go, and to give us real strategies to help us win the game. I had coaches for every sport I did; they pushed me to do things I never thought possible. When I moved to the Big Island, my neighbor was a professional boxer, and he trained many of the UFC fighters in Hawaii. I had been wanting to get back into it, so I signed up and have been training with him ever since. He pushes me to a point where there's no way I can lift or do another pushup, but he doesn't ever let me say the word "can't."

If coaches are beneficial for success in sports, why not have a coach for your business, and for your life? I have many different kinds of coaches. When I was focusing on my weight, I had three physical trainers coaching me. I had a business coach, Kimber Kabell, for years. I remember calling her after my sell-out on the Home Shopping Channel (HSN) to express my gratitude to her and to share my exhilarating experience with her. When you have two people put out the same intentions, they are more powerful. My coach saw me better than I saw myself. She didn't feel the fears I felt, and she didn't hear the negative voices I heard. Her view of me helped open my perspective. It was much easier to succeed when you had someone cheering for you who was on your team. IF YOU CAN'T AFFORD TO HAVE A COACH, ask a friend to help keep you accountable, someone who reminds you of the things you said you would do, an accountability partner!

Set goals with your accountability partner, and check in with each other on a weekly basis. My first coach, Haaheo, helped me set ninety-day goals. I have also used a business coach who helped me set weekly goals, and every Sunday, I would have to submit a report of what I had accomplished. Outside of work, I have met with a life coach at least once a week for the last 10 years to break through any issues I may have at that time.

I am a firm believer that "how you do anything is how you do everything." Whether it is your relationship, or your business, you will repeat the same process and habits. When I learned and grew and became more effective in my business, it would automatically improve my relationships. And when I learned ways to improve my relationships, I would also apply those techniques in my business.

I discovered that when I structured and planned my days ahead of time, I was more likely to do tasks and stay focused. I started booking times in my calendar for fun stuff, like surfing and spending time with my husband. These are enjoyable activities for me, and I wanted to make sure there was always time for them. If you don't schedule it, something else may get in the way!

You can literally plan everything, right down to eating. I have created an eating plan for myself, and I write down what I desire to eat each day. When I plan and prepare my meals, I am more likely to eat them. I'm clear about my eating goals and I make sure everyone around me knows about them so they can support me too.

GOAL SETTING

Recently, I set a five-week goal to get back in shape. I immediately booked a photo shoot at the end of the five weeks; I needed the deadline and some motivation. I posted my goal on Facebook so that my friends and fans could help to keep me accountable to my goal. Then I asked for support! I messaged a physical trainer and asked him if it was possible to lose ten pounds in five weeks. He said "yes" and put me on an eating program.

It's always been hard for me to eat healthy when I travel; I work out and eat healthy when I'm home, but when I go on business trips, I end up eating out and gaining weight. My first business trip on the new five-week plan, was to Vegas for a "Money and You" workshop with Marshall Thurber. Sticking to my meal plan was actually easy, especially with the addition of protein my trainer supplied me with. It allowed me to stay on track while on the road. While on my next trip to Canada to shoot an infomercial, I scheduled times to go to my brother's gym, and he helped me with my diet plan. When I was back in Honolulu, I went and worked out with my girlfriends. It's much more fun when you do it with friends. My Big Island coach was texting me the whole time I was traveling, keeping me on track with my training.

I had a ton of support and a great network of people to keep me accountable. Through the course of my travels, I shared my goal and plan with others. Some of these people desired to lose weight too, so they joined me on the weight challenge. I love inspiring people to get healthier!

Follow these simple principles, and you will achieve all your goals!

Six principles to achieve your goals:

1. Set a goal.
2. Set a deadline.
3. Get someone to keep you accountable.
4. Ask for support.
5. Have a plan.
6. Stay committed!

1. **Set a goal, make it measurable and make sure you have a date.** I desired to get fit within five weeks. If I didn't set a completion date, I would just put it off, until tomorrow, or the next day, or the next day! It's okay if you don't make the date; setting the date just gets you moving forward. You may reach the goal in a few days, weeks, or even months, but you will reach it!

2. **Make sure you have someone to keep you accountable.** Creating an online support group through Facebook, as well as surrounding myself with a great group of offline friends made getting fit more fun. Having friends support me and keep me accountable made the goal easier to reach.

3. **Make a commitment that depends on you reaching your goal.** To keep myself committed and motivated, I booked a photo shoot at the end of the 5 week challenge. I knew that if I was

going to have photos taken of me, I would stay committed to reaching my goal!

4. **Ask for support, and be prepared to take it.**

   I reached out to my support system and coaches. I made sure I had a plan, a trainer, and my support system, so I would be more committed, educated, and prepared. My coaches texted me to see if I'd been working out when I'm traveling and I am now able to make better choices when I go out to eat. I inspire others around me when I eat healthy!

5. **Have a plan.**

   I plan out the whole 5 weeks. I break it down weekly and then daily what I'm going to do in different categories. For example, I plan what I'm going to eat and when. It makes it easy to plan and do. It doesn't leave room for conditioning to decide what to eat. The more clear you are about the plan, the more likely you will be to accomplish your goal.

6. **Stay committed.**

   With all these steps in place it makes it much easier to stay committed. When I find myself deviating from the plan, I say things like "It's only 5 weeks, I can do it." When you find yourself about to give up, call someone for support. No matter what keep moving forward!

I applied what I knew about creating success in business to my personal health and fitness. I had an eating plan, I visualized the end result, seeing myself in the best shape of my life and the beautiful photos I would cherish forever. I surrounded myself with people who had fitness as their passion.

At the end of the five-week challenge, I went to the photo shoot while I was in Vegas for a tradeshow. It was a huge success! That experience created new behaviors that I am committed to continuing in my life. It's all about having balance, and making time for the things you are passionate about. Now, I take the time to schedule workouts and prepare meals ahead of time, especially when I'm working and traveling.

My 5-week challenge photo shoot! I achieved my goal, and I will cherish this photo. (Photo by Steve Wenger)

MASTERMIND GROUPS!

I also have a mastermind group. We have weekly meetings on Skype and each week, we go through our goals and share if we've completed, or not completed, our goals. This keeps us all accountable. It also allows us to enjoy the process and bring attention to all the wins we've had along the way. I'm also one of the founders of Women Power Group (WPG), which currently consists of four women, who are now my best friends. We meet regularly to brainstorm and come up with solutions to challenges and we share our successes. We set goals in all areas of our lives: professional, relationships, health, spiritual. Then at the end, we go out and treat ourselves to a weekend getaway at a spa. My first involvement in a solid Mastermind Group was with a PSI goal-setting group. I was on a team of twenty-five people, and our goal was to support each other in achieving goals. We met every week, and I also had an accountability coach that I called each day to share what I had completed and also specify what my plans were for the next day. The team was a great support in coming up with solutions whenever someone had a challenge. I believe when you have many people putting out the same intentions, it's much more powerful in manifesting your goals. I now have several Mastermind groups going at the same time. Each one provides a different perspective and all of them have benefits!

YOU ARE SO CLOSE!

Together, we create more, because we cheer each other on. When you're climbing a mountain, and someone says "YOU ARE ALMOST THERE, SO CLOSE!" you just give it your all and push yourself just a little more. Find people to cheer you on, and make sure you become the cheerleader for others too! A while ago, I was volunteering at a life success course. There were about eighty people in attendance, split into groups of ten. I would watch them do their event, and when they were almost at their goal, I would say, "keep going; you're so close!" Then I would see a change in their being; they would get focused, and, every time, they would reach their goal. Some would be at a point where they were giving up and had no energy to keep going, but once I said, "YOU ARE SOOOOOOO CLOSE," there was a transformation and they would reach their goal.

I would even do this with new groups who weren't even close to achieving their goals. I said, "You are so close!" and guess what? Even though they weren't even close at all, they shifted and went in the right direction and reached their goal!

There were times when I had no idea if I was close or not to my goal, but once someone said "You are so close," I believed it, and it gave me the extra strength to go a little further, and, most of the time, all I needed was that little more to get to my goal. So, whenever you're feeling stuck, just tell yourself "YOU ARE SO CLOSE," and it will get you over the hump, and, before you know it, you will reach your goal. So many people stop right before they reach their goal. They don't realize the pot of gold is just around the corner. Wouldn't you give it your all if you knew that it was just right there, just ONE MORE STEP TO TAKE? Wouldn't you take the next step?

EXERCISE:
YOU ARE SO CLOSE

Use this technique when you feel like giving up. Be you own cheerleader. Tell yourself, "You're almost there!" Say out loud, "YOU ARE SO CLOSE!" This can give you the impetus to push you toward reaching your goal. Don't give up! Post signs on your walls, doors, and mirrors that say, "You're so close!" These will remind you to keep going!

LEADERSHIP!

I used to think a leader was someone who told a group of people what to do, and I was never really comfortable with that kind of position. However, once I started to follow my dreams and just go for it, I inspired many people around me to do the same. I was their inspiration; they thought that if I could do it, they could do it too. There's a big part of me that loves to help others find their passion. I know that just by living the life of my dreams and continuing to be inspired, I am influencing others, and people will naturally be attracted to me. When it comes to my business, I noticed how recharged people would get just listening to what I'm doing next. When I started my fitness challenge, people around me desired to do the same. It was like they were looking for a leader to follow. I am a leader of self! I take responsibility for my own actions, and, that way, the results I create are from me! I feel that we are leading all the time. How are you leading people and in what direction?

I used to be the quiet one, and I was scared to voice my opinion; I was afraid that what I had to say wasn't important. Also, I often had a fear of being wrong. This kept me from standing up and being a leader. However, I discovered I could be a leader just by leading by example. When I started taking responsibility for myself and had enough courage to take a risk and start my business, my example gave others the confidence to do the same. It inspired others to follow their dreams. I was breaking through obstacle after obstacle like a trailblazer, and many were following me along the path I had cleared. I was just leading by example. When I stood up for what I wanted, people supported me and followed me. They saw me as a leader because of that, and they were inspired by it!

TOGETHER WE CREATE MORE!

There was a time in my business life when I wasn't interested in entertaining investors; I was making money and I didn't think I needed the help. What I realize now is that with the help of investors, I could build my business even faster! Instead of waiting to make the money, then using the money to grow my business, I would have enough to grow right away and grow much faster. Plus, it's not just about the money; when you bring others onto your team, you have more minds working together, sharing the same vision, and you are more powerful! In any team, each person has their own strengths and creative solutions that they bring to the table. There is strength in numbers!

Recently, I entered a Facebook competition and I needed to ask for support from my network. At first, I found it extremely hard to ask my friends to vote for me. I typed out the words, "Can you do me a favor and vote for me?" closed my eyes, and pressed "Send." Then I waited for responses. My friends replied with posts like "Of course. You helped me out when I came to Hawaii. Anything for you!" I was pleasantly surprised by the amazing support I received from my friends. All I had to do was ask. The negative voice that said I was a hassle to them was wrong. So, I asked everyone I knew on Facebook! When it got really tough and I had given all I had, the leaders stepped up and got their followers to post and vote for me. That was a big lesson for me: I didn't have to do everything myself. I could be a leader, and still ask for help because people believed in my cause and my vision; they believed in me.

I continue to apply this lesson in my business every day. I consistently remind myself that I don't have to do it all myself, that I can delegate more to others and that, together, we have the potential to create even more. While I agree that you have to be persistent and work hard to create success, I desire to work smarter, so I have learned to ask for and accept, support.

FOCUS ON WHAT YOU ARE GOOD AT!

As the song goes in *The Lego Movie*, "Everything is awesome, everything is cool when your part of a team. Everything is awesome, when you're living your dream!" Being part of a team is more fun, and it greatly increases your ability to create. You don't have to work hard; you can delegate and focus on what you love doing the most. You can make more money and put in less time. I don't try to do everything in my business anymore. Yes, at the beginning, I had to do everything myself; but once I could delegate, I did so.

I had the opportunity to hear Dr. Ernesto Sirolli from Italy speak live, and he confirmed that I was on the right track. He said we are only meant to do one of three skills: product development, marketing, or financial management. There's not one person who can do it all and be effective. STOP TRYING TO DO IT ALL YOURSELF!

It is more important for me to focus on product development and marketing, rather than focusing on the day to day operations of the office. The more I delegated, the more products I could develop and sell, and the more time I could free up for surfing.

On a recent business trip, I was just relaxing in the hot tub when this gentleman asked me what I did for business. I told him that I invented products for hair care and makeup. He told me that he had an idea of his own. I encouraged him to just follow his dreams and start his own business. I offered to mentor him because I really thought his idea was great and that he had to do it. As it turned out, he had some great ideas for me to grow my business. He was into online marketing, and I was looking for new strategies to take my business to the next level. We both had information to share with each other, it was a win–win situation. I had a desire to help and wasn't expecting anything in return. When you give without thought of reward, you always get back!

NETWORK/SUPPORT!

Marshall Thurber said, "Your network is your most valuable resource." I'm so glad he pointed that out; it's so true. Out of all the resources I have, my network is the most valuable. You can't buy that. Social media is a very efficient and effective way to build your network. When I first started posting instructional videos on YouTube, people started to subscribe to my channel and my network began to grow. No matter how busy I am, social media sites such as Facebook and Twitter allow me to stay connected with thousands. The Facebook competition that I was involved in allowed me to attract like-minded people who were into entrepreneurship. Now, that's targeted networking. My network has taken years to build, and it all starts with the formation of a relationship. Don't forget to tap into your network. You never know; one friend may know of another friend, who could lead to something big. Remember, people love to help!

When it comes to reaching out for support, I'm still practicing to make it perfect. I still feel scared, putting my hand up to ask a question, but the fear doesn't stop me from doing it, and, each time, I risk a little more. But each time, it gets easier. I feel blessed to have created such an amazing network of people. They are there for me when I need them, and they know that I am there for them too. This is very powerful, and extremely comforting. Remember, together we create more!

THE POWER OF ONLINE & SOCIAL MEDIA!

I am so grateful for social media! Up until now, I have not had to invest in marketing because YouTube, Facebook, Twitter, and Instagram have been such powerful marketing tools. When I started my business in 2006, social media was just becoming popular, and I had no idea that it could be used to market my product. When I posted my first video, I had thousands of views in one day. It is now 2014, and I have over twenty million views and I have over 18,000 thousand subscribers!

Many millionaires have been made with YouTube. Billions of views and a huge following results in Google sending successful YouTuber's some pretty hefty checks! I personally know of one person who got

$12,000 for their first monthly check! The Gangnam Style video that went viral and sent Korean rapper, PSY to the top of the charts all over the world has more than a billion views! Now everyone has heard and seen that song! Canadian singer Carly Rae Jepsen and supermodel Kate Upton were discovered on YouTube and reached a lot of people too. Michelle Phan started makeup tutorials on YouTube and gathered a huge following of five million subscribers. Then L'Oreal signed with her and helped her create her own cosmetic line! She travels around the world to promote her products. How inspiring is that? If you have a dream or a talent, YouTube is a great way to get yourself out there. You never know where it will take you, and its FREEEEEEE!

I knew there were plenty of people searching for how-to hair videos on YouTube. All I had to do was make instructional videos of me using my product, and they would end up buying it. At the end of my video, I post a link so they can "click here" to buy it. Another great video tip is to provide a sneak preview of some of your other videos. This gets them wanting to watch more! When you upload your videos, make sure you choose the right search engine optimization (SEO) words in your title for the video. Think of words that people will search for. For example, I wanted to add the words "layers," "layering," and "layered." I made sure I had the most important one in the title, and, in the description, I made sure I used all of them. Thus, I had a title: "How to Cut Layers," and a description: "A step-by-step tutorial on how to layer cut your hair. Now you can DIY and create layered hairstyles. Makes Layering your hair easy at home!" This ensures that when someone searches on YouTube for "How to cut layers," my video will be high on the search engine results.

I HAVE ADAPTED TO CHANGE, EMBRACED CHANGE, AND USED IT AS ANOTHER WAY TO LEVERAGE!

With the Internet, you can reach more people faster! I discovered it organically, and it continues to grow because I'm open. BE OPEN!

Here is the link to my Youtube Channel, please subscribe! https://www.youtube.com/user/creaclip

I love that the Internet allows me to connect with thousands in just minutes. I can post a photo on Instagram and thousands of people know exactly what I'm doing. When I was involved in the Facebook speech competition, I was able to connect with and receive support from thousands of people in just one week. Plus, I got to connect with friends and family who I hadn't seen for fifteen years! On YouTube, people from all over the world see my videos and my subscribers are the first to see a new video once it posts. It takes mere minutes after posting a video before I have thousands of views from all over the world! Start building a following today.

The power of the Internet is amazing and there's so much more that we could be using. More and more businesses are using Instagram for marketing. It's so fast and can reach out to so many people.

What I love about YouTube is that my customers are making their own videos of themselves using the CreaClip and CreaNails! I see them use Instagram in the same way too. Instagram makes it easy for customers to post pictures and hash tag them to CreaClip! It's a good practice to ALWAYS LEARN, GROW, EVOLVE. The Internet makes it even easier to make a difference in the world!

CONTRIBUTION!

It's great when your company is profitable, but it's even more amazing to know that your products or services are making a difference in the world. My dream and my invention started out as a way to help my clients maintain their own hair in between haircuts. Now I get emails from customers saying,

"Thank you so much for inventing the CreaClip. I haven't cut my hair for three years. I can't afford to go to the salon."

"My grandma is in a nursing home, and I used it to cut her hair. Thank you!"

" I have four daughters and this invention saved me so much money already."

"I'm a student, and now I can have trendy haircuts."

It is so great to see customers using my products!

(Photo by Monalyn Gracia)

I never would have thought people would be thanking me for inventing my products, or that I would be able to help so many families. When I get testimonials from my customers, it always comes at the right time. It's always exactly what I needed to hear. I always desire to help people as my way of giving back to the community, but then, every time I help, I always get more back. It's funny how that happens. It can get challenging at times, but I know I am making a difference in the world, and that keeps me moving forward. I know I have to keep inventing. I have many more ideas to come!

CHAPTER 3

COUNTER NEGATIVE THINKING WITH POSITIVE THOUGHT AND ACTION

The power that signals success is the power of your mind.
—Napoleon Hill

I remember so clearly my first martial arts competition in China. When I stepped into the stadium, I could see all of the competitors training. They were kicking the pads so hard that the loud noise that came off the pad scared me! My teacher, Alex, told me not to be afraid; the sound of the pads was a lot louder than it really was; we were in a stadium, so the noise bounced off of everything. But it was too late; I was deep in fear!

WHEN MY ATTENTION IS ON FEAR, FEAR GETS BIGGER!

My teammate was there beside me and said, "Mai, remind me never to do this; I wouldn't want to fight." With this, I got even more scared! When your outside environment confirms what the negative voice is saying, it makes it more believable! Be careful of your thoughts and what thoughts you choose to believe. Also, be selective of who you listen too.

That day, I experienced how being fearful can drain your energy. I had to qualify for my weight category of fifty-two kilos, the lowest weight I ever had to fight in. During the weigh-in, I was standing next to a sweet man from Sweden who was also competing. We didn't say anything to each other until after the competition. When we finally talked, he said that I had the most terrified look on my face that night. Not only could he see but he could also sense the fear radiating from me. Even though I was afraid, I knew that this was what I desired, and that I would grow from the experience. I will explain this concept more in Chapter 5.

The next day at the competition, I was on stage in a stadium filled with 20,000 people. It was like the whole village had come to watch me fight. I did not know it was going to be this popular! The press was there for the big Canada versus China fight, and people had bought tickets to see ME fight! I didn't realize how big this competition was when I had committed to it. I felt like a celebrity. The mayor greeted us at the airport with flowers and gifts, and we had a driver. We were even on the news! The whole village was waiting on the sides of the streets as we drove by. They had banners on all the poles leading up to the stadium; it felt like I was in the Olympics! They had been preparing for this for over a year.

The sound of the loud pads was in my head that night. I had created this story in my head that I had no chance. I had already made up my mind that I was going to lose. I had used up all of my energy, being consumed by fear and anxiety. Because I was nervous and scared, it was no surprise that I lost the first round. However, in the second round I won, so I got to fight another round. It was close... but I lost in the third round. After the match, I thought to myself, "It wasn't that bad, she wasn't that much better than me, and, if I had been on my game, I would have won. The stories I created with my fear were not true at all!

That experience taught me that my thinking could affect my results. Each time I competed, I would know the night before if I were going to win or lose. If I was positive, I would create positive results. If I was negative, I would create negative results. If I had any fear or doubt, it really affected my performance! However, this didn't stop me. I continued to compete again and again, and I only lost two of twenty matches. I even placed third in a world competition in Shanghai!

During the fights I won, my friends said that I had the "eye of the tiger." I couldn't stop laughing, but it was true. I was so determined and focused, just like in my hair competitions. I was present, clear, and I would go on to win all of Canada. But when it really mattered, I would lose because of the pressure and uncertainty. I wish I had known back then how to manage my fears better.

Win or lose, it didn't matter. That first competition in China was an amazing experience. The following morning, we were sitting in the hotel lobby and there was a newspaper on the table. There I was on the front cover! I couldn't believe it. Even though I lost, I made it on the front cover of the morning news!

*Making the front page of the morning news made
losing my first competition feel like a WIN!*

When I returned to Canada, I was featured in the local newspaper also! My parents were proud of me. I inspired my older brother to get back into martial arts, and we ended up traveling to Florida and competing together. It was nice to bond and spend time with him. He was a great fighter and he did very well in the competitions too!

I was an award-winning hairstylist by day and a champion kung fu fighter by night! It was great doing all the things I loved.

At one of the competitions, I met some foreigners who told me they were training in Beijing. One of my goals was to train in Beijing, so I expressed my desire to one of the guys.

I FOCUSED ON WHAT I LEARNED AND TRUSTED THAT THIS EXPERIENCE WOULD LEAD ME TO THE NEXT.

I had reached a plateau and I needed to keep growing. The next step was to go to China and train with the best! This would fulfill my need for travel, as well as help me improve my Mandarin! I enrolled in the Beijing Sports University for three months, and I was going to be training all day in taolu (forms) and sanda (full contact fighting). My boss Roy was understanding and supportive of my new adventure. He was really the best boss. He had paid for half my tuition for advanced hair training and he supported me in my hair competitions. I'm so grateful to have had such an amazing boss. When you are involved in a team that supports you, the sky's the limit when it comes to creating.

When I got to Beijing, I stayed on campus in the dorms with all the other foreigners. I made friends from Australia, England, Poland, and elsewhere! Training was intense; I had to condition myself. We trained for three hours in the morning doing taolu, and, in the afternoon, everyone took naps. Then it was training again for another three hours with the Beijing sanda team. It was the best time of my life. I had so much fun training and speaking Chinese, and everything was so cheap. You could eat out or get a massage for just two dollars!

My three months went by so fast. I had an around-the-world ticket, and was encouraged to travel to different countries, but I decided to extend my stay in China. During that time, there was another world championship competition in Shanghai I was training for. Besides myself, six other students from the Sports University enrolled. We all took the train overnight to Shanghai and competed together. As soon as we arrived at the stadium, they pulled me aside and told me I had five minutes before the match. I was shocked. I didn't even get to warm up. I had only enough time to wrap my hands. I was fearful that I would hurt myself by fighting without first warming up. I was all over the place. I got thrown on the platform, and, because I wasn't focused, I lost that match. I was so angry; it seemed so unfair.

I used my angry energy to get back on track. The next match, I fought against a girl. I gave her the evil stare, and, in my mind, I thought, "I'm going to destroy her!" And I did just that. Each time she came, I side-kicked her and she fell to the ground. Two times, I even threw her off the platform. I kicked her in the stomach so hard, she fell. There was no way I was going to lose that match. My friends sent me photos of the event, and I was staring my opponent down; I looked mean.

I ended up winning third place in the Shanghai match! Winning a match against the Chinese was a big accomplishment. It was such a great feeling.

WHEN MY INTENTION IS STRONG, NOTHING CAN STOP ME.

I'm so certain that people can feel the energy when they are around me. That's what you need to do, BE CERTAIN! When I'm not focused and have self-doubts, it really affects my performance.

BEFORE YOU GO INTO A COMPETITION OR A MEETING OR AN IMPORTANT EVENT, GROUND YOURSELF AND GET CLEAR.

I always take a few minutes to get centered, breathe, bring my attention to now, and let go of whatever I'm holding onto that happened in the past. I then visualize what I desire to create for my future.

EXERCISE:

VISUALIZE AND CREATE

In the morning, before you get out of bed, take a few minutes to visualize yourself being successful in all the activities you have planned for that day. If you have an important meeting, see yourself being relaxed and cordial and accomplishing agenda items quickly. If you desire to find a new car, picture the perfect car with a great deal price. It also helps to play out in your head the things you have planned for the day, and this makes it real easy to manifest. Don't forget to thank the universe in advance for manifesting your desires and success. And in the evening, when you review your successful day, thank the universe again.

When I was on HSN, I would take twenty minutes and play it all out in my head like it was really happening and say all the things I desired to say. It's the same with fighting; I would visualize myself winning. When I was practicing for my speeches, I would go for daily walks, during which I would run my speech in my head and act as if I were in front of people. I didn't say it out loud but just kept talking in my head and letting it flow. I already knew basically the outline of what I would talk about. It was all in my head; so I could go on stage and speak from my heart. It was almost like the universe was channeling through me. I used to say that I was excited to see what would come out of my mouth!

DON'T BELIEVE THE NEGATIVE VOICE INSIDE YOUR HEAD.

We all have them—negative voices. It's a struggle every day and every moment to shift my thinking from negative to positive. I still have those negative voices, but I choose not to let them hold me back, and it gets easier each time I do it. The most negative voice always tells me that "it's not enough." This Negative Nancy tells me I'm never doing enough, I'm not capable enough, and I won't have enough in the future; I'm just not enough. Each day, I would hear some kind of sentence with those words, "not enough." But now, because I'm aware, I can really identify and shift my attention to the opposite—that there is enough, there's abundance, and that everything is perfect just the way it is. And I won't lie; it's not always easy, but now I'm able to shift my thinking more quickly. Before I knew that this negative voice was a liar, I would really believe that I was not enough. I would think it was reality. I got really good at distinguishing between my intuition and my conditioning!

Whenever I find myself in a difficult situation and I feel like things might not work out, I simply keep moving forward. I have always managed to turn things around and these experiences have helped me grow dramatically. My products were a huge success selling on HSN, but after that, I did not sell anything for a whole year. I began to worry. Under an exclusive contract, I feared not holding up to my end of the bargain and worried that I wouldn't make it.

WHEN YOU ARE IN FEAR, INSPIRATION CANNOT EXIST.

I make a point to shift my energy into a better space, so I can receive guidance from my intuition or the universe. I used to think I was not successful, but everyone around me thought I was. I didn't consider myself successful unless I had made a million dollars but my husband brought to my attention, "Just selling your product on HSN is a huge success! How many people do you know who can say they've done that?" He was right, I had a lot to be proud of, and it was time to celebrate all the little things that I had accomplished. I started to own my success and see myself as even more successful. That's when the money started rolling in, and now I'm making millions! When you feel like you already have it, what you are seeking for will manifest! In the movie, *The Secret*, they say, WHEN YOU COME FROM A SPACE OF ALREADY HAVING IT, THE UNIVERSE GIVES YOU MORE.

POSITIVE THINKING!

My first experience with the power of positive thinking occurred in my mom's booth at a local flea market, where she was marketing her own designs: a collection of sportswear and exercise clothing. I noticed people would come into our booth, look around and then leave without buying anything. They would ask questions and then just leave. After some time, I started to assume that this pattern was going to keep happening.

My mom said, "Mai, get up; the customer is here." I said, "I don't need to get up. They aren't going to buy anything; they just look and then leave." My mom was furious. She said, "Leave my booth; I don't want that negative energy around. How are we going to sell anything if you already think people are not going to buy?" It was a huge lesson. I could see how much that affected my mom; it was like I had killed her dream. From then on, I dare not be negative when I was in the booth!

As an adult, I am very aware of the power of my thoughts, and I practice positive thinking each day. I wear a beaded bracelet, and each time I catch myself thinking of something negative, I shift a bead and think of the opposite or a positive thought. I would count my shifted beads at the end of each day. This simple exercise really helps me practice positivity and create new behaviors that will last. It takes ninety days to create a new behaviors. The more you do anything, the more natural it will become, just like martial arts!

NOTICE WHAT YOUR ATTENTION IS ON!

I became so aware of my thoughts, and it made it very obvious where I was focusing my attention. Each time I fought with my husband, I would say, "This sucks; we fight all the time," and he would say, "Why do you think that? Out of the twenty-four hours in a day, we fought for twenty minutes." I thought, "that's true; we don't fight all the time." Yet my attention was only focused on the one thing that went wrong that day. I forgot to notice all the good things!

I realized I was focusing on things that were either wrong, or not enough. Then I would feel horrible. I would shift my attention each time I noticed I was going to that "not enough" thinking. I would think about what was good, what I was grateful for. Most of the time, the little "wrong" things were not worth focusing my attention on. When you focus your attention on something, it grows. If I think we always fight, we will fight more, and if I think we have a strong, healthy relationship, we will. Use this principle to your advantage, and grow positivity instead!

BEING PRESENT / FEAR OF FUTURE!

I practice being present in my life and I focus on what is happening right now, even though I have a long-term vision. From a day-to-day thinking process, I try not to project too much into the future. I stay focused on the now. Do you ever fear that something bad will happen in the future? My mind often wanders and starts thinking of crazy things that might happen in the future. I catch myself creating things out of fear and I think they're really going to happen. Fortunately, I am able to bring myself back to the present moment where everything is awesome. DON'T WORRY ABOUT THINGS OR EVENTS UNTIL THEY REALLY HAPPEN. When you think too much of what can go wrong, it holds you back. IF IT'S NOT A PROBLEM NOW, DON'T WORRY ABOUT IT! Plus if there's ever a problem you will come up with a solution when needed.

To help me with my worries, I use a simple mental trick. I tell myself that if it's not something critical, I will save that problem and worry about it…on Wednesday. I call Wednesdays WORRY WEDNESDAY. I save up all the little issues and worry about them on Wednesday. Most of the time, everything I thought I needed to worry about would work itself out by then, or didn't even become an issue. Let go of your worries by writing them down and placing them in a mental or physical box, labeled "FOR WORRY WEDNESDAY."

FEAR DOESN'T EXIST IN THE PRESENT!

There can be a lot of fear and worry leading up to any challenge, but when you're in the present moment and doing what you love, fear does not exist. FEAR IS ONLY AN ILLUSION, because all we have is the present… the now. Fear is only a projection of what we think *might* happen in the future. Since the future is unknown, and not set in stone, your fear is not reality, it is a creation. FEAR is an acronym for False Evidence Appearing Real.

I see the connection so clearly now. When I was doing hair for a client, I was in the zone, and solely focused on the present moment. I would be thinking about how amazing my haircut would look when I was done, so I wanted just to listen and not talk. To the clients I was close with, I just told them I needed to focus on their hair, and I would prefer they talked. Most of my clients loved telling me about their day, or their challenges with their significant others, friends, or children.

I am in the zone when I do hair, martial arts, surfing, dancing, speaking; I'm present. Fear does not exist because I am in the moment. When I speak to groups, I'm just being me; things just seem to flow and whatever comes out of my mouth is what was meant to come out. It feels as if the universe were flowing through me.

I was talking to my stepson Ethan, who's twelve. I asked him, "Do you have a negative voice in your head? He said, "Yes." So I probed deeper. "What does it say?" He said, "It says I can't do things. Sometimes, it tells me I won't like certain foods before I even try them. But to be honest, 90% of the time, I love the food, even when it says I won't like it."

Ethan even gave the negative voice a name, "Bad Bob." How brilliant! Why not give it a name? It helps you identify it more and distinguish "it" from you.

EXERCISE:
NAME YOUR NEGATIVE VOICE AND OBSERVE IT

Give your negative voice a name: Worry Wanda, Anxious Annie, Fearful Fred, Gloomy Gus, Doubtful Dan, Negative Nancy, etc. Make a resolution to take the next step toward your dreams, and just observe the ways your voice tries to talk you out of things. Realize that this voice is not you; it is your ego. Dis-identify from it and notice it, but don't listen to it. It will only tell you lies.

Ethan was so smart! He said, "Sometimes that voice becomes more believable when my friends at school say the same thing the voice says. Like if I think I'm stupid and some kid also says I am, I start believing it."

That's so true! Surround yourself with positive people because, otherwise, you might buy into others' negativity, and that can really drag you down.

We all have negative voices; we don't need our environment to be negative too. The voices (I also call them ego, conditioning, or programs) are there, and I have so many of them, but I grow from them. Those negative voices may try to talk you out of what you desire. You may catch yourself saying things like, "I want to start a business, but I don't think I'll be able to do it," or "I just don't have enough experience for that job", or "I want to move to Hawaii, but I just don't have enough money." That negative voice is attempting to talk you out of what you really desire! Do not allow it to succeed.

THOUGHTS!

I have many thoughts every day, and, often, there are negative voices that point out everything I do wrong, stating why I shouldn't have done this or that, or how, if only I had done *this*, things would be different. Life would be so much easier with only a positive voice cheering me on!

I have a practice whenever I have a negative thought, to direct my attention to something opposite or positive. I think of something great that is happening. I notice when I direct my attention to what I'm grateful for, I start to feel happy, and when I have gratitude, I'm more inspired and it's much easier to manifest what I desire. I know that whatever I'm thinking about or focusing on, I manifest. Anything that I could ever desire, if I get it in my mind, becomes a reality.

I know this is true for the opposite, so if I fear something bad is going to happen, I create that too. So why not think positive thoughts! Marshal Thurber said, "If you are feeling love, integrity, responsible, etc., you can't feel fear." Fear can't coexist with love because you can only feel one or the other. It's almost impossible to feel inspired if you are feeling angry or resentful. This is why I always try to clear any resentments I may have so I can move on. Resentment has really held me back!

THERE'S ALWAYS A SOLUTION
TO EVERY PROBLEM

PERSISTENCE is the key to successfully batting obstacles back
that life catapults in your way. This is the weapon that causes
enemies such as fear, doubt, and negativity to crumble.
—*Sharon Lechter*

I trust that any obstacle that presents itself to me has a solution. I BELIEVE THERE'S A SOLUTION FOR EVERY OBSTACLE. This way, instead of being stuck, I go right into solution mode. And it's true; I really do find a solution for everything. It's important to know that there can be more than one solution to every obstacle. So, I don't stop once I find a solution. Instead, I ask, "Is there a better one?"

I remember clearly walking with my coach, David, when it dawned on me that if I could continue to find solutions to my obstacles, I would achieve my dreams! It was the thought process behind it. It didn't matter what it was or what I did; if I had that mindset, I would eventually get there, every time! I felt such a relief that day.

COMMIT TO YOUR DREAMS, AND THE IDEAS
& SOLUTIONS WILL COME TO YOU.

This was definitely true for me. I was kind of stuck... I had my prototype and patent, so I was committed; but now what? The next day, I received a flyer in the mail about a "How-to-Invent Seminar." Receiving it was no coincidence; it was exactly what I was asking for! I shouted out loud, "Thank you Universe; you work fast!"

I went to the seminar and it was very inspiring. The instructor was a local inventor, who happened to be a single mom. She successfully invented, manufactured and marketed her own product, and she inspired me. What an amazing connection my instructor was. I learned the ins and outs of inventing from her, and she connected me with her manufacturer and a professional prototyper, and then everything started to move fast!

In the development stages of the CreaClip, while I was trying to perfect the prototype and the packaging, I became aware of a competition at an upcoming tradeshow; they were looking for new inventions. The top ten inventors would get to be on a TV show! This was an excellent opportunity for me to market my product. Entering that competition was a huge motivation, as it gave me a deadline. The competition was in Pennsylvania, and both my working prototype and the packaging had to meet me there because of timelines. Time was tight, but I had faith.

I had a similar experience during a martial arts competition. I realized too late that my passport was about to expire, and my flight was in just a few days. I panicked and then called my coach. He was very calm. I asked, "How come you're not stressed?" and he replied, "Well, I just find a solution! It's real simple; we pay a rush fee to get it processed in four days, and we are stopping in Vancouver for the competition there first, so we can have it FedEx'ed there. We don't need your passport until we leave for China after the Vancouver competition anyway; so it will all work out." It was such a great lesson.

THERE'S ALWAYS A SOLUTION.
INSTEAD OF GETING STRESSED,
FOCUS YOUR ENERGY ON FINDING SOLUTIONS!

At the tradeshow competition, I anxiously awaited the arrival of my two packages. Without my prototype and packaging, this competition was a bust! Thankfully, both packages arrived on time; however, there was a problem with the prototype. The level liquid inside of the product had leaked out during shipping, leaving no air bubble in my level! How would I possibly display my product without this? I immediately called my coach Haaheo for support and advice; she advised me to act as if everything were okay. She said, "Well, maybe the judges won't notice; just act like nothing is wrong." I said, "Okay, you're right; I'll do that."

If I had been worried about the level being broken, I wouldn't have been able to truly pitch the benefits of my incredible product. Instead, I focused my attention on imagining that everything was perfect, and that is exactly what happened. The competition was great! There were thousands of people and it was such an exhilarating experience. When it was time to pitch my product, the press and videographers came to me. There was so much attention on me, and I felt really good. I believed I was going to be chosen; I only had to be in the top ten!

When I got in front of the judges, they loved the CreaClip, and they all wanted samples! I took that as a good sign.

When you have a deadline, it motivates you to get everything in place, on time. That tradeshow competition spurred me to get my prototype and packaging done quickly.

Now the CreaClip was ready for production!

The next step was to make the molds.

Waiting for the results of the competition over the next two months was torture. I decided to keep moving forward to make the time go faster. I was introduced to a networking forum called CEO Space. The founder, BJ Dorhmann, was in town, so I got to meet him in person. He loved my product and said that he could connect me with Bob Circosta, "The Billion Dollar Man." He was TV's ORIGINAL Home Shopping host and helped create the multi-billion-dollar TV home shopping industry!

I was so excited to be presented with this opportunity. I was going to let the universe decide my fate. If I didn't make it on the other shopping network, I could always go to CEO Space and get on HSN.

I knew that I was going to reach my goal and it didn't matter what avenue I would take.

Two months later, the results from the tradeshow competition were in; I was one of fifty finalists… out of thousands of entries! But had I made the top ten? They made me wait another couple of weeks for the results due to the overwhelming demand. Unfortunately, I wasn't chosen. I was disappointed, but I was not discouraged. I knew the universe was leading me the right way.

My next stop was Los Angeles, to visit the CEO Space Forum. What an amazing week it was! I got to meet patent attorneys, branding experts, graphics designers: any professional you could need for your inventing business. I loved that I could meet with them for free and see whom I resonated with. I found everyone on my team there! I met my new patent attorney, my business coach, my branding expert, and even got connected to Bob Circosta! It really fast-tracked my business.

I revisited LA to attend a strategy session with Howard Lim on branding. That's when we came up with CreaProducts! I wrote out my vision and mission statements for my business. It wasn't just CreaClip any more; I had to continue empowering my clients though my Creative Products.

My coach, Kimber, helped me set weekly intentions, and I was so productive and on purpose. When you have a coach, you are more likely to stretch yourself and accomplish more. I signed up for Bob Circosta's University to train as a spokesperson. I needed to be able to pitch my product so we could get it on HSN! Things really started to roll quickly now. Bob and his team took great care of me. Not only did I learn how to pitch my product, they represented my product to HSN, and I was able to get on HSN faster than if I had pitched it myself.

HSN loved my product and contracted me to be the spokesperson! I was happy, and then I was afraid. Perhaps it would be better to have a professional spokesperson? At least they would know what they were doing! I was afraid of public speaking. I had to discuss my fears with Bob. "I'm still scared of public speaking and you want me to go on TV live in front of millions? NO WAY! This is way too scary." Bob pushed me to do it; audiences loved having the inventor on the show. I knew I would do whatever it took, so I accepted the challenge in spite of my fear.

My fear of speaking did not hold me back from taking the next step!

I spent days and nights practicing. I would visualize myself on TV and rehearse the features and benefits of my product over and over. The one thing I was sure of: I was going to sell out on HSN! It was a whole new experience for me. I had airings at 1 a.m., 3 a.m., and 7 a.m., all late-night airings, but it didn't matter to me because the time difference was six hours ahead and I was jet-lagged anyway. I felt like a celebrity!

Sitting in the green room, getting my hair and makeup done was so exciting. A spokesperson came in the room and said, "Hey, did you guys see that new product? You can cut your bangs with it!" I needed that positivity boost! The makeup artist replied, "Yes, I'm doing the inventor's hair right now."

They were very professional at HSN and I was impressed with their staff. I had Bob and his team coaching me all the way through. When I was on air, it was like I was in another place. I was in the zone and loving every minute. I couldn't believe the stuff that came out of my mouth, I said, "Your cousin, your husband, even your sister can cut your hair with the CreaClip!" So catchy! I was just talking the whole time. There were three cameras in the front and sides, and a screen that projected B-roll footage. I had to talk to each camera when the red light was on, and then pay attention to see if they were showing B-roll, in which case, I had to refer to what was on the screen. On top of that, I had to interact with the host and cut hair at the same time! Talk about multitasking.

Before I knew it, the host said, "Oh, we're in the red zone; we are sold out!" She had to cut the airing short and hinted to me to get off the stage because we were done. As I walked off the stage, it hit me. I shouted, "I did it, I sold out! Wow!" Then I jumped up and down and screamed, "Wooh wooh!" to myself, forgetting that I was still wearing a microphone! I looked at the screen and saw the host look up all confused, and he said, "Oh, that's Mai; she just sold out of her product!" It was so cool; you can watch the video airing on YouTube!

That was a moment I will never forget. All the hard work had paid off. I was on fire! I had taken one step, and then another and another, and I just kept going and going, until I achieved my goal!

Here's the link to the sold out video of me on HSN: https://www.youtube.com/watch?v=XUjNcAkZ_P4

I called my family to share the good news. I also called my coach to tell her that I hade made it to the red zone, meaning there were too many callers and not enough people to take the orders! We celebrated on the phone. I was on a high for days! I still had two more airings., and the producers wanted to know if I had any more inventory I said, "Yes, but I already sold out, I want to keep that status. If I go back on, It wouldn't be considered a sell out." Bob and the team said, "Mai, we are here to sell as much product as we can!" On the second airing, I sold out again, selling over 5,000 units in 13 minutes!

I went back and sold on HSN every couple of months for a year. Each time I went, I stayed at a nicer and nicer hotel! I was flying every couple of months for business, so I got elite status, meaning each time there was available seating, NWA would upgrade me to first class; basically, every time I flew, I was in first class! I felt like I was in the big leagues, like a celebrity! Each time I went to HSN, I was able to stop at home in Calgary. It was cheaper, it made the flights seem shorter, and I got to see my family every couple of months. Each time I flew home, I had tears of gratitude in my eyes.

GRATITUDE BRINGS MORE GRATITUDE.

I stopped for just a few moments to ponder how amazing my life was. I was living the life of my dreams, and I got to spend more time with my family. Everything happened so fast that I didn't stop to see how amazing it really was. Wow, was it ever! I made more money in 13 minutes than I did working a whole year at the salon. I had an idea and I brought it to market.

I was in a state of gratitude, so I attracted more abundance and opportunity. This is a fundamental principle of the law of attraction, explained in the movie, *The Secret*.

WHEN YOU ARE GRATEFUL, LIFE GIVES YOU MORE THINGS TO BE GRATEFUL FOR. GRATITUDE BRINGS MORE GRATITUDE.

I was at the airport when I got a call from Bill, my sales rep at America Invents. Bill said, "Mai we have a top infomercial company interested in licensing your product!" What great news! I had desired to have my product featured in mainstream retail, as most products only last on HSN for a year. My time was up, and a new opportunity awaited me.

The next step was to find a company to market my product through an infomercial, and then roll it out in all the major stores. I envisioned having a marketing and distribution professional who could take my product and make it big! The projected sales were in the millions in each quarter, and though my royalty would be a small portion of that, I would still make millions!

They flew me to Miami and hired a top producer and director to shoot the commercial. When I got there, they showed me the set they were building. Can you believe they built a whole set for my commercial? It was like they were filming a movie! Everything was top of the line; they had three hairstylists and two makeup artists. They showed me comp cards of all the professional models, and I got to choose which ones to use. All I had to do was just provide direction on how the hair had to be done! For once, I didn't have to do the hair; I even had an assistant and my own director's chair. Seeing everything come together, I still couldn't believe how amazing everything had been. In just two short years, I had a salable invention and I was shooting my very own commercial.

It cost $120,000 to produce the commercial, and it was top quality. They spent months editing, and, since we had signed an exclusive deal, I wasn't allowed to sell my product to anyone else. This was a very stressful time, as I didn't have any income. Everything was riding on this commercial. Finally, the commercial was done.

When I saw it, my intuition told me that the commercial was missing the pitch: it was for family; it was to save money! They re-edited the commercial quickly, but they had to air it and test it because we had scheduled airtime. When they tested the commercial, it didn't sell. They tried to re-edit the original commercial, but my gut was saying they would have to reshoot the entire thing, and that would be too costly.

To make a long story short, they retested it and, again, it didn't create the results we were looking for. So they came back to me and said, "Mai, you have a great product, but it's just not for TV; we wish you the best of luck."

I was devastated. What was I going to do now? The voices were saying, "See, this is the end of your dream, now you got to go back to Canada and live with your mom." That voice sounded so real that I believed it. I even told my boyfriend at the time that I would have to move back, but he thought I was just being silly. How was I going to pay my bills?

I had no income coming in, and the sales online were really slow. The negative voice said, "Your product sucks; it's a failure." But then I thought, "How can that be? I sold out on HSN; people bought it and loved it, and they have given it great reviews. How can it be my product? It must be the commercial." I called my sales rep and told him, "Bill, I really don't think it's my product." He said, "Mai, it's definitely not your product; it's the commercial." That was a relief. I had been ready to blame myself and the product. So, instead of thinking this was the end, I started to think creatively.

MEDITATION IS IMPORTANT.

Meditation is such a great practice; most successful people have done some kind of personal development, and they meditate! When I meditate, I sit quietly on a cushion and I clear my mind and prepare myself to receive the big insights and solutions that come to me while I am in this state. My mind is quiet, I am present, and this receptive state allows the universe to drop any insight or solutions into my mind. When I'm fearful, solutions don't come; I can't be inspired when I am afraid.

WHEN FEAR OR ANGER EXISTS, THERE CAN'T BE INSPIRATION.

When our roof started leaking and the new roof was going to cost $30,000, I had a huge meltdown. We already had a lot of debt; we did not need this. I really thought this might be the end. I started to send all kinds of panic emails, trying to remedy the situation. My intuitive self said, "THIS IS NOT WHAT YOU SHOULD DO! Wait at least twenty-four hours before you make any decisions or do anything." I had to email people back and explain my panic attack the next day. That was slightly embarrassing.

Rule #1: Notice the voices, but don't panic.
Rule #2: Meditate! Sit on the cushion until it passes!

When I am clear and centered again, I take care of the problem! I no longer make reactive decisions. I sit on it for a few days and then, when I'm centered, I ask if this is what I really desire. If I really do desire it, I will still desire it in the future, and when I take time to be centered, I'm in a clearer state of being. I remember my dad singing the Bobby McFerrin song "Don't Worry, Be Happy." He always had that light attitude. When I thought there was a problem, he would sing that song, and it really helped me let go. Thank you, DAD!

DON'T WORRY, BE HAPPY!

I thought I would have to be successful or make millions before I could be happy, but I realized that if I kept thinking that way, I would never be happy. If I kept looking to external outlets as sources for my happiness, I would never find it. Why wait until I have a million? What if I could just be happy right now?

There's always a solution, and that night at 3 a.m., I awoke with the solution. My 3 a.m. inspirations were becoming commonplace, and great ideas would often come late at night.

EXERCISE:
IDEA AND DREAM JOURNAL

Keep a journal and pen on your bed table. Before going to sleep, think about a problem but don't worry about it. Just say to the universe, "Thank you for coming up with the solution to this problem. Just wake me up when you have it." You let go of it and put it out to the universe. Then you can sleep peacefully. When you wake up with an idea, quickly jot it down in your journal and go back to sleep. Don't start thinking about the logistics of the idea. Just stay in a receptive mode, waiting for more ideas. Write down any dreams too. Some inventions were the result of dreams. The next day, look over your ideas and dreams and use them to solve the problem.

My 3 a.m. great idea was to make videos and post them on YouTube. In the morning, I called my friend Kaoru and asked if she would like me to cut her hair again. She came over. I just wanted to have a little fun with this video, and I wasn't going to try to shoot for perfection. I've watched tons of videos on YouTube; most featured girls in their bathroom, living room, or kitchen doing just real videos. I thought I'd try the same.

So I set up my camera, had Kaoru stand in front of a mirror, and I started videotaping. It was so unprofessional; you could see me in the mirror, holding the camera sometimes when I didn't notice I was in the shot. But it didn't matter because we had intended just to have fun with it.

We started filming and I was the director. "Okay flip your head over, clip the CreaClip in your hair, slide it down and... okay, stop. Now cut!" Kaoru had that worried look on her face again. She whispered, "That much?" It looked like a lot of hair, so she was freaking out, but I said, "Yes, just do it!" and gave her that look of hurry up. So she said, "Oh, okay," and started cutting. All this hair came off, and when she slid off the CreaClip, the hair fell in beautiful layers all around her face, and it took less than sixty seconds! She was so impressed with the cut; she flipped her hair back and forth!

Capturing this live on video was so real. Even I was shocked at how beautiful it was! I decided it was time to cut my own hair. It was the first time I had ever done that layered technique, but it made mathematical sense; and the result was perfectly layered, face-framing cuts in the comfort of your own home. It can even create V-shaped layering in the back, which is hard to do even for an experienced hairstylist. But my product did it all in one shot, in just one cut!

We posted the video on YouTube, and within seconds, I got two views. We watched the views climb, and, in minutes, there were fifty views! We checked back in an hour and it had climbed to 1,000 views. I said, "Who is watching this? I can't believe there are actually people watching my video, and they're interested!" That's when I noticed the comment section. One said, "OMG, I was about to die when I saw all the hair that got cut, but then I was amazed at how beautiful the hair was!" There were so many positive comments about how people just loved the cut. I tried to reply to them all, but it just got out of hand, and, in just a few days, we had over 3,000 views. I kept checking back and it went up to 30,000 views, and then it went viral! I didn't know who was watching, but people loved it and must have been forwarding it to their friends. Can you believe that now this video has millions of views? Here's the link:

https://www.youtube.com/watch?v=TvSdAKKksgQ

The video was working, so I decided to make more videos of different cuts, different hair textures, and I used different models! I called up all my friends and asked if they were interested in cutting their hair. Everyone wanted to be a model in my videos. I now have over sixty videos with 20 million views. My customers and fans have also started creating their own videos with my products. They have created some really cool cuts that even I didn't even think of. CreaClip videos emerged from all around the world, and no matter what language was spoken in the video, the CreaClip was the star, and a video is worth a thousand words!

Bloggers contacted me to review my product. Soon, blogs about my product started to spread! But that's not the best part. Following the post of my first video, I noticed a big jump in my sales. It went from $300 a month to $3,000 a month! Wow, what a huge increase! I was jumping up and down with excitement. Then, the next month, it kept going to $6000, and then $10,000. I called my mom and said, "Mom, sales were $10,000 this month!" I couldn't believe it. Then it kept growing. When it was $20,000, I started making jokes like, "Dad, you don't have to work anymore!"

Imagine, for three years straight, sales increased from $30,000 to $75,000 a month. I was making millions in sales; my dreams had come true. I desired to make money in my sleep, and now I was doing it!

Now, I'm not a very analytical person, but when the sales started to go up, I started making graphs. I had a graph for daily sales, monthly sales, and yearly sales; I had all kinds of color graphs. My friend Jim, who is a very analytical person, asked me if I did the graphs when he was visiting. He was impressed! He had never seen that side of me before. It was such an amazing time in my life. All the hard work paid off, and I was glad I never gave up. I trusted the Universe and myself and I kept moving forward no matter what.

I had created an online following on YouTube, and I was at the top of the at-home haircutting industry!

It was FREE to market my product videos on Youtube, and in addition, Google sends me a check each month, from the Google Adsense program, which allows advertisers to post ads on my videos. My Google checks were between $500 and $1,000 a month, not a huge amount compared to some other YouTubers like PSY, but I loved the passive income! Each time a Google check arrived, my husband and I would treat it as free money and buy frivolous things we desired. I bought myself another surfboard! One can never have too many surfboards! We make a day out of it and celebrate our wins!

The Youtube videos have also attracted distributors from all over the world, and my products are now being distributed by companies in Germany, France, Australia, South Africa, Netherlands, Norway, Italy, Canada, and elsewhere!

Even the celebrities were using my products; Amanda Rigetti from the TV show *The Mentalist*, Lauren Velez from *Dexter*, and even some of the cast from *Twilight*! In 2008, I was finalist for best new product of the year, and, in 2011, I won an award for the fastest growing business!

Winning "Best New Product of the Year" was a highlight for me!

Two years later, the past CEO of the marketing company that produced the infomercial called and admitted that they totally missed the mark on the commercial. He was with another company, and he wanted to know if we would be interested in licensing again.

When I was less experienced, I needed them, but now that I had things working, I decided to pass. There were other infomercial companies interested, and we turned them down as well.

I decided to produce my own infomercial and test it one more time. This time, I directed the commercial. I found a video production company in Los Angeles who charged me a fair price, and did an amazing job. We had a casting call and got to choose the perfect models. I hired a media buying specialist to sell the commercial to the media and channels to help produce the commercial and campaign. We spent months putting it together. It aired on TV for two weeks on some really big channels: E Channel, Oprah Network, and Disney!

It was amazing to see myself on TV!

Suddenly, it hit me—my invention just aired on OWN; I couldn't believe it. At that time, I was still living in Honolulu, where the houses are extremely close to one another. I was in my bedroom, and I could hear the "CreaClip" commercial. I ran next door to my neighbor and asked, "What channel are you watching?" She said, "Oh, I PVR'ed Oprah. Hey, are you the inventor of the CreaClip?" I said, "Yes." She said, "Oh, I saw the commercial on OWN and HSN when it first came out; I'm always watching HSN." I couldn't believe it; what a small world! It was an amazing experience to see my product featured on such big TV channels. After weeks of airtime, the results came in.

Again, we didn't get the results that we needed to make it profitable. We shifted our focus to more family-oriented channels so we could target moms. OWN and E Channel had been expensive and it was hard to make a profit when we were spending so much on media. We selected some lower-cost media and ran another test. Unfortunately, the owner of the media buying group I had hired had been involved in a lawsuit and was forced to shut down. They owed me money for media that we never had a chance to test; the Spanish version of the commercial. I took this as a sign that I wasn't heading in the right direction.

So, I focused on what was working, and I put more energy into making videos and growing my online following, and my business kept growing and growing and growing!

Had I given up when the first infomercial bombed, I never would have created this incredible success. THINGS REALLY DO HAPPEN FOR A REASON. When I look back, things played out perfectly!

IF ONE DIRECTION IS NOT WORKING, I JUST TRUST IT'S HAPPENING FOR A REASON AND FOCUS ON WHAT IS WORKING!

There's always going to be challenges. I just learn from them and move on. I don't get stuck on what I should have done and beat myself up for my mistakes. Instead, I focus my energy on what's next, what I can do to turn it around!

My business was doing really well. I took the time to celebrate all the little things. Enjoy the journey along the way; I loved the whole process! If I didn't enjoy myself along the way, it wouldn't be worth it. I desired to have fun while creating success, not create success and then have fun. When you have fun doing what you love each day, you can never regret anything.

I had worked hard for five years, so I decided to take a break and focus on my health and my relationship. My partner and I went to a silent retreat in California and our relationship jumped to a whole new level. I even broke through my fears about getting remarried.

I was divorced and I always thought that as long as I never remarried, there would be no chance of getting divorced again. That thinking was not working for me. I loved my boyfriend, and, had I not been divorced once already, I would have married him in a heartbeat. I was holding myself back out of fear; I didn't want to be hurt again. I had one foot in and one foot out of my relationship, and I realized that I needed to have both feet IN for this to work.

I'd rather love fully and risk getting hurt than not give him all of my love. I didn't want to live in fear any longer. I changed my thinking and released the fear! If I did get hurt, I knew it would only make me stronger, so I had nothing to fear.

My heart desired to commit and marry him, so I jumped in with both feet! We went to a justice of the peace, just the two of us, and we did it for all the right reasons! It felt great to just go all in and give it my all. We'll host a formal ceremony for our family at some point (when we can get them all together in one place), but, for now, our marriage is a symbol of our commitment to each other.

I also made my personal health a priority. When I started my business, I was going real hard. I would work for hours and lose track of time. When you are doing what you love, time flies and you may find yourself always wanting to do it. I was so focused and excited, I wouldn't take the time for stretching breaks, or spend time with my significant other. I knew I could have it all, and I desired more balance in my life; great relationships, great health, and a great business! I was really enjoying myself and I even managed to surf once or twice a day. Life was great! I had freedom to do whatever I desired when I desired it. Eating out at the best restaurants with my friends was my way of thanking them for supporting me, and was also a way to celebrate my victories. I always wanted to be able to take care of my parents, since they did such a great job taking care of me; so I treated them to a vacation in Korea. It felt so good to be able to do that!

INTUITION!

A large part of finding solutions to problems is the ability to listen to your intuition and to distinguish the voice of intuition from the voice of conditioning. I am so good now at listening to my intuition; I can't take the next step unless I'm really certain. It's hard for me to not take a step if my intuition is screaming, GO FOR IT! It's like building a muscle; the more you use it, the stronger it gets.

My intuition guides me in my choices, and many good business decisions have been made when I am grounded and coming from center. The decisions I make in my business and my relationships are not based

I always make sure I have a healthy balance of work and play in my life!

on fear or conditioning. I desire to be with my husband, and this is a choice from my heart, not a judgment. I desired to be with him not because I needed to be or should be, I just do what feels good. When I make decisions that affect my health, like what to eat or put into my body and my environment, I do what feels right, not what my conditioning tells me.

In University, my intuition was screaming ACCOUNTING IS NOT IT! When the opportunity to become a hairstylist came, my intuition yelled GO FOR IT! When my back hurt doing hair at the salon, and I daydreamed about my invention idea, my intuition hollered GO FOR IT! My intuition is so loud and clear now that I can't avoid listening to it.

WHAT DOES YOUR INTUITION SAY?
WHAT DO YOU DESIRE? WHAT IS YOUR DREAM?

HOW DO YOU KNOW WHETHER IT'S
YOUR INTUITION TALKING OR YOUR CONDITIONING?

A big sign for me is when the voice in my head takes on a sudden urgency and tells me to take action right away…hurry, do something, quick, react now! When I hear that voice, I hold off and do nothing. I just sit with it, and when I'm calm, I revisit the subject and see what I desire to do, not need to do. Something happens when I get fearful. I feel like I need to do something right away, and when I do act, I usually have to go back and fix it. It's better to wait and let it sit with you before making any big decisions to take action.

Another sign I listen for is the word "should." For example, when a voice tells me, "You should keep working at this job because it's good money and it's stable or it's easy." "SHOULD" is always a big sign for me that I'm not doing what I desire. Usually, "shoulds" are someone else's values that I'm trying to live by. Similar words are "need" or "have to"; they have the same effect as "should."

CREATING NEW BEHAVIORS!

When you learn something new, always apply it right away and over and over again, until you create a new behavior. Repeating the new behavior often will help that behavior become a natural response. The same thing happens with your mind; if you continue to say positive affirmations, you will one day believe them. It's so important to notice the negative words you say to yourself. The other day, I caught myself saying, "I'm so stupid!" I immediately corrected myself, saying, "Actually, I am intelligent and creative." The words you say to yourself *do* affect your thoughts and actions.

Another exciting part of the PSI seminar I attended was the daily affirmation. For ninety days, everyday, I said, "I am a sexy, hot, powerful leader, confidently living my dreams now!" At that time, I didn't believe one word; I was actually very uncomfortable saying I was sexy because I didn't own it. After ninety days of saying it, I believed it! Now, I actually OWN every word of that contract.

EXERCISE:
CREATE A NEW YOU!

Grab a piece of paper and write down "I am" followed by four to six words describing qualities that you desire more of. It can be anything you feel you are missing in your life, or something you'd like to improve. If a word feels uncomfortable, it's okay, but write it down anyway. For example, "I am beautiful, perfect, courageous,healthy, and confident."

Repeat your sentence out loud every day, and repeat it more often when you are feeling doubtful. Post your "new you" statement on your bathroom mirror or on your fridge as a gentle reminder of who you really are.

CHANGE YOUR BEHAVIOR
TO CHANGE YOUR CONSCIOUSNESS.

Changing the way I think automatically changes my behavior, and I am able to make different/better/smarter choices. Once I learn something new, it's hard for me to make that choice again because I know it does not serve me. My intuition won't allow me to go down that same path because I know better.

When I first started my business, I conserved expenses by taking care of the customer service and bookkeeping myself. A small change in my awareness and thinking made me realize that I was actually holding myself and my business back by not letting go and delegating those simple tasks. I realized I could be making more money if I hired someone to do it. After I had that awareness, I never went back. I made business decisions that made me more money. Attending personal growth seminars and business workshops are extremely valuable, and when you apply the information you learn from them, it can provide a great return on your investment!

IF YOU CHANGE YOUR BEHAVIOR,
YOU CAN ALSO CHANGE YOUR CONSCIOUSNESS.

I know it takes ninety days to create a new behavior, so if I desire to change my thinking, all I need to do is do it for ninety days. It becomes a new behavior with new thought patterns!

I have used this with the procrastinator voice that tries to talk to me often. That voice says "Do it later, you don't want to do it now, it's complicated, and it's going to take a long time." It would get me to put things off. I would end up with a to-do list a yard long, I'd feel overwhelmed, and things would never get done.

I desired to break that pattern. Each time I heard that voice tell me to "do it later," I would practice a different behavior. Instead of putting it off, I would do it right away. I told myself, "you don't have to get the whole task done, just take one step, a little step; just spend ten minutes working on that task." When I put the time requirement in, the voices telling me it was going to take too long really didn't have any validity.

Switching to this new behavior broke the procrastination thought pattern. I would hear "later" and I'd practice doing it right away. Most of the time, I was able to get the task done in those ten minutes, or I would find out that the task was rather easy when my procrastinator voice made me think it was really difficult. Once I started the task and got into it, I sometimes ended up spending more than ten minutes on it, but I managed to finish the project. It was a great way to prove conditioning wrong. I created a new behavior, and, in return, I had a change in consciousness.

You can do this with anything. WHAT THOUGHT PROCESS WOULD YOU LIKE TO CHANGE? What behaviors would you like to change? When you change one or the other, you create different results!

EXERCISE
WHAT THE FUDGE!

What if you have a habit that you do so infrequently that it happens only a few times in ninety days? What then? Suppose you have a habit of saying the 'F' word, but only when you're stressed and emotional. You want to replace it with a less vulgar word like "fudge." What you can do is shout "FUDGE!" while doing vigorous exercise like martial arts. Even though you may not be stressed and emotional, your heart rate will be increased as it would be when you're emotional. So you would condition yourself to say, "fudge" when you're emotional.

CHAPTER 5

FEAR IS A SIGN THAT YOU'RE ON THE RIGHT PATH

Always do what you are afraid to do.
—Ralph Waldo Emerson

When I first started out in martial arts, there were no girls doing Sanda, so I had to train with the boys. It was tough for sure, but some of the boys were so handsome! The teacher was impressed that this foreign Chinese *girl* from Canada desired to learn, and it encouraged them to scout girls from all over China to train with them. Of course, they had to pick the toughest girl in China, Lili, to train with me!

When I first met Lili, she had short hair, and she was tough and very manly; however, she was the sweetest girl. We quickly became good friends, but in the ring, it was all business. I remember her picking me up, just like on the wrestling shows on TV, and she would throw me down on the floor! Man, did that hurt! I had to ice my body after each session. We trained eight hours a day, and, in between, all I could do was rest and keep heat packs on me, so I could be ready for the next training session.

I was not about to give up. I knew the more I practiced, the better I would get. I was always preparing for the next competition. I had

Mai preparing for the next competition!

often heard that the bigger the risk, the bigger the reward of personal growth. For one year, I made a commitment to myself that whenever I had resistance to taking a risk, I would do it anyway because I knew I would grow from it.

FEAR IS A SIGN THAT YOU ARE HEADING IN THE RIGHT DIRECTION.

Often, people would ask me to speak at business presentations and share my success story. My natural reaction was to say no, because I was afraid of public speaking. Most people are. In fact, a 1977 study asked 3,000 people to list some of their fears. The fear of standing up in front of an audience was the most frequently cited fear. Since public speaking was something I was reluctant to do, I would not have the energy to do it. But, I realized that because conditioning had resistance to it, it must be something that my heart would desire to do. I was just afraid. Fear was a sign that it was something I desired. When you don't desire something, there's no fear involved, just noninterest; it's clear that you just don't desire it. If you didn't desire to do it, there would simply be no energy associated with it. So, when you feel resistance, it's a sign that

Mai faces her fear of public speaking, even on TV!

you should look deeper. Yes, there are times when fear arises and it is valid, like jumping off a cliff, and no, you shouldn't be compelled to do it. When your heart wants to do something, and your ego is stopping you, be aware overcoming this fear usually leads to growth!

The year I committed to "just do it" whenever I was afraid, I said "yes" to many public speaking invitations. Each time I would be so stressed, and I would hear all kinds of negative voices in my head prior to taking the stage I expected that I would be really nervous when I spoke; instead, I actually enjoyed speaking and I grew from the experience. The fear leading up to it was so intense that I just assumed I wouldn't enjoy actually doing it! Never make assumptions!

IF THE FEAR WEREN'T THERE, WOULD YOU LIKE IT?

One time, I told my coach, David, that I wasn't a fan of public speaking, because I felt like throwing up every time! He said, "Maybe it's not the speaking that you don't like. What if you had no fear?" It's true. If I didn't feel like throwing up, I would enjoy public speaking even more. I knew there was something I needed to overcome: my fear of public speaking. Each time I accepted an opportunity to speak, I stretched myself a little further, and it got easier. I got better at it, and the fear got smaller.

THE MORE YOU DO IT, THE EASIER IT GETS.

When you practice not being afraid, you will not be afraid any more.

One of my biggest challenges in public speaking came during the 40th Annual Principia Conference competition. They had the top inspirational speakers from all over the world sharing their message and knowledge; Bob Proctor, Dr. Demartini, Mark Victor Hansen, Lisa Nichols, and others from the movie *The Secret* were there. They were my mentors; they inspired me, and I had been learning from them. I desired the opportunity to share the same stage with them.

When a friend told me about the competition they were having, I was all over it! I desired to share my message with others and inspire them to follow their dreams. This was my chance to inspire many. To win the competition, you had to get the most votes on Facebook for your video. I stayed up all night editing my video and I was the first one to start.

I won the competition and earned an opportunity to speak on stage in front of 500 people and then I suddenly realized I was afraid of public speaking! I went to Toastmasters once and I never returned because I was so scared. I also realized I didn't have a lot of experience as a speaker. I had spoken at business presentations from 30 to 100 people, so that gave me a little experience, but I had no formal training. I already knew I DID NOT NEED EXPERIENCE TO BE SUCCESSFUL. I always felt fear before going on stage, but this time, I just stayed in the moment, remained present and trusted that I could do it. I spoke positively to myself, saying, "I've got this, I'll be perfect, and I'm just going to be authentic and be myself." I knew the message that I wanted to get across to my audience, so I felt confident about my content!

When I was on stage, everything just flowed! I was back in the ZONE; I was on fire. When I'm in that state, there's no fear. Stuff was flying out of my mouth and even I was amazed at what I was saying. I even joked about how they gave Bob Proctor a clock to keep time while speaking, but where was mine? It went by so fast.

YOU DON'T NEED TO HAVE EXPERIENCE OR NEED TO KNOW HOW; you just have to have a clear intention and GO FOR IT. Without any experience, I went straight to speaking in front of 500 people and sharing the stage with my mentors. It felt amazing. I was so inspired, alive, and motivated afterwards. I couldn't believe I had done it. I sure proved those negative voices wrong; I can be a speaker and a good one, too!

EXERCISE:
WRITE YOUR FEAR LIST AND FACE ONE

Make a list of everything you would do if you weren't afraid of doing it. Don't list scary things if you don't have an interest in them, like skydiving. After you write them down, pick one and just take one step! You can start small and build confidence. PICK ONE THING YOU ARE AFRAID OF, TAKE A SMALL RISK, AND COMMIT TO IT! This will really push you to grow! And you might discover a new passion!

I couldn't believe my message had such a huge impact. Someone else said, "Mai I didn't expect you to be so good! You were better than some of the featured speakers who have been speaking for over thirty years!" Now that really hit me. I never would have thought that was possible until I actually did it. Now that I know I am capable, I know I can be an inspirational speaker.

In my vision statement at the Ike Pono Quest in 2010, I wrote that in ten years, I would love to be an inspirational speaker, but I was so afraid of public speaking that I thought I could never make it happen. I was always the shy one who never spoke up. Whenever it was time for Q & A, I wanted to ask questions, but I was too scared. It was so draining to hold back, I was fighting in my head: What should I say?

*Sharing the stage with my mentors in front
of hundreds of people was exhilarating.*

Is what I have to say important? But when I found my voice and just spoke, it was so much easier. That speech at the Principia conference proved I could do whatever I put my mind to!

Fear of doing something is really a sign that it's something I desire, and THE BIGGER THE FEAR, THE BIGGER THE GROWTH. The times I risked the most were the times I got the biggest results. I choose things that I am afraid of and do them, knowing that they are opportunities.

I know that I'm heading in the right direction when I'm afraid; it means that I'm growing, that I'm getting uncomfortable. If it were comfortable and safe, then I would be doing more of the same and staying in one spot. This allowed me to get outside my box and experience something new. It seems easy to play it safe, but the truth is, it's actually easier to do the things you fear when you don't have that fear anymore; you feel empowered and inspired. When people tell me they are afraid, I remind them FEAR IS A SIGN YOU ARE HEADING THE RIGHT DIRECTION. Just trust it and wait and see. Each time it was true for me.

EXERCISE:
COIN FLIP

Here's a little exercise I do when I can't decide between two things; I flip a coin. First, you will need to decide what will be heads and what will be tails. Pay attention to your thoughts before you flip the coin, are you leaning one way or the other? Now, flip the coin and then stop. Close your eyes and notice your thoughts. Then, open your eyes to reveal the results. Notice how you feel about the result.

Most of the time, before I even flip the coin, I already know which one I'm hoping it will be. What could that be trying to tell you? I used this technique when I couldn't make up my mind about quitting the salon. Heads was, "I quit my job" and tails was "I stay working at the salon." Before I flipped that coin, I could feel that I was hopeful it would be heads! Once I flipped that coin, but before I opened my eyes, I took notice of my feelings about the outcome. When I opened my eyes, I became acutely aware of how I felt when I saw the outcome of my flip; was it sweet relief or a twinge of disappointment? That day, my flipped coin answered me with "heads, I quit my job!" and I was ecstatic. If it had landed on tails, I would have felt disappointed. My disappointment would have been a sign that my real desire was to quit my job.

Remember, your decision is not dependent on whether your coin lands on heads or tails; this exercise is not like a fortune teller showing you the answer through the flip of a coin. It's all about you tapping into yourself so you will be able to clearly see your next step. Try it!

IF YOU HAD A MILLION DOLLARS, WHAT WOULD YOU DO?

I love asking people this question, and I love hearing their replies! So, what if YOU had all the time and money in the world, what would you *do*?" I remember one of my new friends replying with, "I would love to build furniture. I don't even care if I make money; I just love doing it!"

When I chose a career in hair styling, I didn't care whether I was going to make money or not as long as I was doing what I loved every day. Life is too short not to enjoy each day; it's too short not to live the life of your dreams. If I love each day, I know that when I look back in twenty years, it won't matter where I am, because I will have loved every moment of getting to wherever I end up.

THE DESTINATION IS NOT THE REAL PRIZE.

Follow your passion. If you are true to what you value most, true to what's most important to you, you will always create success. I love what I do, so when challenges arise, I am more likely to break through them and I'm more willing to go through the pain and suffering of the challenges because there's nothing else I would rather do! Work also doesn't feel like work to me; it's definitely more like play. I'm just as excited about working as I am about surfing; when I wake up, I'm excited to look at my work emails. I'm on fire and I'm organized because I'm passionate about it. When you love doing something, it really doesn't feel like work! Confucius said, "Choose a job you love, and you will never have to work a day in your life." When you experience "work" that doesn't feel like work, it is divine.

FOLLOW YOUR PASSION AND YOU WILL BE SUCCESSFUL!

When I had found my passion in hair and became successful with that, I desired to explore other things that I was passionate about, which lead me into Chinese martial arts, surfing, and inventing!

If you desire to make money doing what you love, you have to find a way to exchange your service or product for money. The greater the need for your product, the more you will get paid.

My husband, Jason, recently started following his passion for photography! (Photo by Chris Hirata)

MANIFESTING FAST.

When I am in alignment with my dreams and my purpose, things happen really fast.

For twenty years, I desired to get a tattoo. For ten of those years, I couldn't decide which tattoo to get. I was analyzing this way too much! When I realized I would be fifty if I waited ten more years, I finally grabbed my opportunity and did it; I got a huge tattoo and I love it!

Don't spend the next ten years before taking the next step, thinking, "How should I do this? What if I fail?" It doesn't need to perfect, and you don't need to know everything.

JUST GO FOR IT, AND DON'T WAIT TOO LONG OR THE OPPORTUNITY WILL PASS YOU BY.

There are times when opportunities are presented, but because I'm not clear on what I desire, I don't see them; I don't know what I'm looking for.

BE CLEAR ABOUT WHAT YOU DESIRE.

If you don't know, how will the universe be able to give it to you? When you know with certainty, the universe can manifest it almost instantly. That happened to me a lot; I would attract what I desired, and fast too! I always say, "Thank you, Universe! That was fast!"

Before our house deal on the Big Island was finalized, I would stare at the photos of the house and dream about how amazing it was going to be to live there. I put out a vibration to manifest that home.

When I applied for the mortgage, the loan officer said he had everything he needed and everything was good to go. But when it came time to close the deal, the loan officer was not prepared and said I wasn't able to qualify for the loan. My heart sank, but I reached out for support, and a friend's husband, who specialized in mortgages, assured me I could get the loan. Within three weeks, I had my loan approval and I was certain I was going to get my dream house!

ARE YOU STUCK OR NOT GROWING ANYMORE?

Do you feel bored and not challenged in your life? Do you wonder what your life would be like if you just GO FOR IT? Do you really desire to take that step, but you're afraid? Do you desire to follow your dreams, BUT you just don't have enough money, or you think you don't know how, or think you can't do it? Are you worried you will fail?

If you hear yourself saying "I want to, BUT...." that means you want to do it, but you're afraid. The word "BUT" is a sign for me that I actually desire it. If I didn't really desire it, my words would be simply, "I don't want to do it." I often hear the word "but" followed by reasons people are afraid. Don't worry; this is normal.

What are some things that would challenge you to get outside your comfort zone and do something different? To create different results, you have to do something different! If you didn't see things as risks, what would you do?

EXERCISE:
IF YOU HAD A MILLION $$$$!

Another exercise you can do to find out what your purpose and passion is to ask yourself, "If I had a million dollars and lots of time, what kind of business would I do?" Don't ask what you would spend your time and money on. People who win the lottery and suddenly have millions of dollars waste it. Ask what you would love to do if you were living the life of your dreams. Most people don't go after their dreams because of lack of money; lack of time is number two. But if you had lots of time and money, then you would just do whatever you loved to do! What is it?

28 MidWeek July 23, 200

ENTREPRENEURS *Linda Dela Cruz*

A Hairstylist On The Cutting Edge

With a snip here and a snip there, Mai Lieu will demonstrate her do-it-yourself haircutting product, the Crea Clip, on the Home Shopping Network for the second time in August.

"I appeared on the show in February, and we were sold out in minutes," says Lieu, who has 15 years of experience as a hairstylist.

> **❝ I created this product to help customers do it themselves. ❞**

Lieu created the product because her customers would cut their own bangs and she'd have to correct what they did because it was too short or uneven. The Crea Clip can cut bangs, create layers, trim long hair and cut men's hair.

"Bangs should be cut every three weeks," notes Lieu. "I'd tell my clients that I'd cut their bangs for them no charge, but no one has time. So I created this product to help them do it themselves, since they are doing it anyway in between haircuts."

product into local stores.

"I've loved inventing since I was little," says Lieu. "When I was 8 years old I came up with an idea — two years later I saw it selling and I thought, 'Hey, I thought of that.' It's happened many times. So I didn't want to let this idea go. I had a burning desire to do it."

Lieu tried out her product a year ago on Oprah's competition for the Next Big Idea, and out of 6,000 people she made it to the semi-finals. But she didn't continue because her product was still a prototype.

"That experience helped me tremendously," says Lieu, who has been working on the product for three years.

"I knew I wanted to do this, and the universe has been on my side," she says. "If I was thinking I needed some packaging, then the next day someone who does packaging would call me. I've stayed positive because I know whatever obstacles have come up, there are solutions."

Her plans include inventing more products for hair and other uses.

For more information, call 818-230-7644, or log onto

Mai Lieu demonstrates her invention, the Crea Clip

Take risks! If you do nothing, nothing will change.

WHAT DREAM CAN YOU MAKE COME TRUE? What is it that you desire so badly but you are afraid of? If you had all the time and all the money, what would you do? What would you do for free? I believe you know what you want. If you had it your way, what would it be? Take that risk; you have nothing to lose. Even if it turns out not to be what you expected, at least you tried. Don't live in regret; the life of your dreams is waiting for you!

VISION!

Everything begins with a vision. When I had the idea for my first invention, it was not just a product idea. The vision was a sort of business plan, a course of action that was more than just one product. I envisioned creating the product, selling it on TV, and then writing a book to share my message with the world. I tell people I had an idea for an invention, but really, I had a vision for a lifestyle.

WHEN I HAVE A VISION, IT'S BECAUSE I REALLY BELIEVE IT, AND THEN THINGS MANIFEST. Things happen; I attract the right people and opportunities show up. Because I'm really clear, I'm able to see the opportunities in front of me, and, of course, I have to take action! It wasn't until after I created all the success that I realized that it was a direct result of my vision. A good friend messaged me one day and said, "Mai, I just wanted to let you know you have inspired me and I am now finally quitting my job and starting my own business. You told me 9 years ago when we first met, that you had an idea for an invention, and I had no doubt that you would do it. And you told me you would one day write a book and inspire others. And here, you did it all!" I had a vision, a passion, an intention, and I just kept taking the next step. You too can re-create your life based on your passions and your desires, and it feels good!

A few years into my business, I went to a Vision workshop called Ike Pono Quest, and the exercises included writing my five-, ten-, and twenty-year visions. The facilitator said, "Write down what you desire, even if you think it's impossible."

I wrote down my desire to be an inspirational speaker so I could help others follow their dreams. I was scared of public speaking, but I knew deep down that I could break through that fear if I wrote it down and committed to doing it. Some of the visions I wrote down at that seminar are already manifesting in my life! I also did a workshop on Master Planning with Dr. Demartini for one year and I looked back and noticed that 80% of the things I wrote down have come true!

EXERCISE:
WRITE YOUR VISION!

Write out your five-year, ten-year and twenty-year visions. What can you see yourself accomplishing in five years? How about ten? Or even twenty? That's a long time and you could be really productive in that time…so stretch yourself, push your limits, open your mind and let the impossible be possible! If you think it can happen, it will, so dare to dream in this exercise. Don't forget to review your vision in five years and compare it to your reality.

EXERCISE:
DREAM BOARD!

When you finish writing your vision, make it visual by translating it into a dream board! Put images of all the things you desire on that board. You will want your vision board to be visible and you will want to see it often. Choose a spot that will inspire you and your family without intruding on your space. The amount of space you have for your personal "dream board" will determine what medium you use to create it. Your dream board can be an oversized piece of paper on the wall, a bulletin board, cork board, or just your bare wall. Seeing your dreams as pictures helps you make those dreams more vivid and real in your own mind, and those images will stay in your subconscious. I actively use vision boards to keep me on track with all my goals. As you achieve your goals, you will need to set new ones, so be on the lookout for that next step…your next inspiration!

One of my vision boards. Never stop creating.
When you can see your goals, you can achieve them!

Another exciting learning experience for me was starring as an extra in the movie "Shanghai Noon." They were filming in Calgary, and my brother and I played the parts of coolies, building railroads. My kung fu teacher, as well as some of the more advanced kung fu students, were cast as stunt doubles for the movie. That experience made me think I could become a stunt double too! Starring as an extra meant I would have a tiny shot at meeting my inspiration, Jackie Chan.

I just love the Universe. I had an opportunity to stand right next to Jackie in a scene, and during a break, he even started a conversation with me! He asked me, "Are you a Canadian-born Chinese?" I said, "No, we came to Canada when I was four." I even had the opportunity to tell him about my kung fu background. He touched my shoulder while we were talking, and I had a big smile on my face. I desired so greatly to have the opportunity to meet him and then I was fortunate enough to have a conversation with him. "Thank you, Universe. That was fast!"

Now, I don't believe in coincidences, but I do believe that everything happens for a reason. Several weeks later, Jackie Chan *happened* to drop by my salon, looking for a brush. I *happened* to have my kung fu newspaper article at work, because I was going to laminate it that same day. When Jackie came in, I went up to him and said, "Hi! Do you remember me?" (I don't think he remembered me.) I reminded him of our conversation on the set, and he immediately relaxed. I asked him to sign my newspaper article, and he did! How cool is that! He could have gone to any salon that day to buy a brush, but he came to the one I was working at. I believe it was my energy that attracted him to that salon!

Photo Caption: Jackie Chan signed my newspaper article!
(I'm on the right)

IF YOU DESIRE SOMETHING, START VISUALIZING AND FEEL IT. YOU NEVER KNOW WHAT, OR WHOM, YOU CAN ATTRACT!

EXERCISE:
VISUALIZE, FEEL, ATTRACT

Think of something you strongly desire to have or do. Now visualize yourself having it or doing it. Don't just see it, feel it as if it's really there, as if it's really happening. Experience it with all your senses. If you desire to eat out at one of your favorite restaurants, envision the smell and taste of your favorite dishes. Hear the music and babble of conversations while you're there. Feel the ambience. Give thanks for it, and you will attract its manifestation.

ALL YOU NEED IS CLEAR INTENTION, FOCUSED ACTION, AND YOU MUST NEVER GIVE UP!

Sometimes, people really don't know how close they are to succeeding and they stop when they are just so close. I believe THAT LIFE ONLY GIVES YOU THE OPPORTUNITIES YOU ARE READY FOR. What opportunities are being presented to you that you aren't taking? You would not be presented with the opportunity if you weren't ready for it, and you wouldn't have your energy focused on it if it wasn't something you desired. So, embrace it, be open, get clear, and commit!

Have you ever been at a party when you're feeling tired, low on energy, or just not very talkative, but then someone starts to talk about one of your passions. You automatically perk up with energy! Your passion is your life force. It will stimulate you and energize you. Sometimes, I have a hard time waking up in the morning and I just feel sluggish. As soon as I open my work emails, I get a sudden burst of energy, and I'm wide-awake and engaged. I love everything about my business, it brings me energy and I really enjoy it. Wouldn't it be nice to love what you do so much that it energizes, stimulates, recharges and refreshes you everyday?

CHAPTER 6

ACHIEVE
FINANCIAL LIBERTY

Financial freedom is a mental, emotional,
and educational process.
—Robert Kiyosaki

If you want to get out of the rat race, you have to either start a business or invest in real estate, and if you can do both, that's even better! As I created wealth in my business, I began reinvesting my wealth, so I could make more money, instead of adding more assets, like boats and fancy jewelry. I desired financial liberty. I desired free time to do whatever I pleased. I desired to have the option to surf all day if I so fancied. I desired to have money to fly home to Canada to visit my family. I desired to never worry about money.

I also thought it wise to create multiple streams of income. That way, if one stream was down, I had another to back me up. Plus, business can be risky, and I knew better that to put all my eggs in one basket.

I have watched many successful business owners make a lot of money but spend it all and end up with nothing! My goal was to create financial liberty; I want to choose to work because I desire to and not to pay the bills.

When I was a child, my parents made some successful real estate investments; they were smart and they lived the life they desired, but they also invested into other things so their wealth was working for them. Of all the investments my parents made, their investments in real estate were the ones that made them the most money. One of the properties my parents owned was set aside specifically as their retirement plan, and they liquidated it once they were ready to retire. I thought this was brilliant! I was inspired to learn more about real estate investing, and growing my wealth, so I attended workshops to learn more. I loved Robert Kiyosaki's and Sharon Lecher's teachings, the authors of *Rich Dad, Poor Dad*. Robert is an entrepreneur from Hawaii, who made a majority of his wealth in real estate, and Sharon specializes in financial education for entrepreneurship

Like my parents, I wanted to enjoy life, but I also planned to save and invest my money! An abundance of foreclosures screamed "opportunity" to me, and, since I already had money saved up, I started buying houses on the mainland. Rather than buying one house in Hawaii for a million dollars, I could buy several homes on the mainland. The rental income I got from the houses I owned paid for themselves, as well as the rent for my house in Honolulu and for my other living expenses. I was financially free! I was living in a million dollar property with no mortgage!

When making real estate investments, I always envisioned purchasing property that I would live in, but it didn't make sense to mortgage a million-dollar home and add the stress of a $5,000 mortgage payment each month. The way I did it, I was still living in my dream house: I just didn't own it. I had the lifestyle I desired, I was debt free, and I was financially free.

When the economy was low and there were a lot of foreclosures, I advised others to buy real estate! Investors always say, "Buy low and sell high." I knew this was the perfect time to buy. Even if you already had a mortgage, it made sense to get a home equity line of $50,000 so you could buy two foreclosures and start renting them out. JUMP ON OPPORTUNITIES AS THEY COME UP, OR THEY WILL PASS YOU BY. Now that the economy is bouncing back, I am thankful that I invested when I did. WHEN YOUR HEART SAYS THIS IS A GOOD INVESTMENT, TRUST IT AND TAKE ACTION.

Being successful in real estate is all about timing. When I bought my first condo in Waikiki ten years ago, I bought just in time. and I was ready when the opportunity came up. I had been planning and saving for this opportunity, so when it came up, I took action. Six months later, my property increased in value by 30%.

When it came to investing, I took baby steps, rather than diving in head first. I didn't start off by investing $100,000. I started with $20,000, then worked up to $30,000 and then $50,000. I didn't go out and buy a million-dollar home. I took ONE STEP AT A TIME, AND EACH SMALL STEP LEAD TO ANOTHER! Once I had confidence in my investments, I started looking for larger investments opportunities.

I invested my money in stocks and I invested some in foreclosures. Then, I bought the home of my dreams on Big Island! I made sure that all my investments would cover the mortgage. For three years, I desired to invest in vacation rentals. I looked into real estate in Maui, but nothing jumped out at me. I knew the right investment would come. I was patient.

DONT RUSH, WAIT AND LET THE UNIVERSE BRING YOU THE OPPORTUNITY.

I kept researching and I waited until my intuition screamed "This is it!"

I WAITED UNTIL I WAS REALLY CLEAR AND CERTAIN. I put out a desire to the Universe for a condo in Waikiki that I could turn into a vacation rental. This way, when I visit Honolulu, I will always have a place to stay! I kept looking and looking, until the opportunity fell into my lap. I had a friend with a condo in Waikiki. Years ago, I told her that I also desired a condo in Waikiki. She "happened" to be selling her condo, and the opportunity just felt right, so I WENT FOR IT! I was the proud owner of a vacation rental in Honolulu! My vision was to have several properties, and, so far, I have added three properties to my estate in just one year, including an oceanfront property in Kona! I plan to have properties all over the world. I am really excited and passionate about vacation rentals. I don't do anything unless I find passion in it. KEEP FOLLOWING YOUR PASSIONS AND KEEP CREATING!

MAKING CHOICES FROM CENTER NOT FEAR!

Each time I have a new awareness, I make different choices, and, if my awareness is centered, the choice I make could earn thousands of dollars. On the other hand, a choice made from fear could cost me thousands. I am very conscious about whether the choices I'm making are from center or from fear. The choices I make can really affect my business! If I'm operating from a sense of lack in my business, I make choices that are not as effective. But if I'm coming from center and know that there's abundance, I make choices that create more. I experience this each time.

A while ago, I thought about starting a dog-boarding business. I thought it would be a great way to supplement my income, and fostering dogs was a way for me to give back. We provided a home for the dogs and helped them get adopted into loving families. I enjoyed it at first, but after five months, I was frustrated by the amount of work this involved.

My vision was to create freedom from work, and this business was going to do the opposite, and take up too much of my time. Fostering the dogs was an excellent opportunity for me to see all the drawbacks of the dog boarding business and I realized it was not what I truly desired. I asked myself, "WHY AM I DOING THIS BUSINESS?" I needed to be clear on whether it was in alignment with my vision or not. My life transforms each time I become more aware!

My awareness led me to another stream of income that I called CreaART. I had always dreamed of selling my paintings, and this stream allowed me to do just that! In grade 2, I used to draw my friends, and they loved it so much. I had requests from students daily for drawings, and some used the drawings as gifts for Mothers Day!

In high school art class, my teacher said, "Mai, you are really good; you should become an art teacher." She thought I had so much talent. I knew that I was really good; it just came natural. I could create with ease; it was like I could see things and just put it on paper or mold it into art. When I was older, I still enjoyed art, but I knew it would be difficult to create the level of success that I was striving for.

The hair industry was my perfect compromise; it's a very creative career, and I could make money easily doing hair. Doing hair was my form of art. I was the artist, and molding people's hair came natural to me. I was able to see the hairstyle that would fit each client perfectly and then create it, even if I wasn't trained to do that particular style. I was a free-flow hair cutter. I would cut one piece and check it, and then cut another. Doing hair was like molding clay in art school, which is part of the reason I loved hair so much. When I competed in hair shows, I loved up-dos the most; preparing hairdos for classy evening events was exciting. Creating works of art with hair was my specialty, and I won first place two years in a row at the Alberta Beauty Competition.

COMPETITION WINNERS

These are some of the winners of the 2001 EDMONTON SHOW COMPETITIONS. They put their technical and creative abilities on the line for all to see and judge and came up winners. Make the decision that this will be your year to shine. Make the commitment to compete in the Edmonton ABA Show competitions. Perhaps your name or photo will appear here in the year 2003.

WOMEN'S FASHION CUT & STYLE
1st Place Winner - Lise Benson - THE MANE DOOR
2nd Place Winner - Artine, Ghazarian - ALTIMO HAIR GROUP
3rd Place Winner - Sandy Roberts - SALON ON SIXTH

MEN'S IN-FASHION CUT & STYLE
1st Place Winner - Hung Van Ngo - JEROME HAIR SALON
2nd Place Winner - Frank Lombardo - HAIR INFINITY
3rd Place Winner - Kelly Ann Oneschuk - PROPAGANDA

NEW TALENT WOMEN'S FASHION CUT & STYLE
1st Place Winner - Amanda Mendys - THE MANE DOOR
2nd Place Winner - Curt Nestman - SALON ON 6TH
3rd Place Winner - Mariam Al-Mousa - DELMAR COLLEGE OF HAIR DESIGN LTD.

EVENING ELEGANCE WITH LONG HAIR
1st Place Winner - Mai Lieu - BIANCO & NERO
2nd Place Winner - Barbara Christen - THE MANE DOOR HAIR STUDIO
3rd Place Winner - Hung Van Ngo - JEROME HAIR SALON

Creating works of art with hair was fun and rewarding.
Doing hair was an artistic outlet for me.

So, as another stream of income, I was inspired to create and sell art. Wyland Art and my CPA told me that Robert Nelson's originals went for $100,000! If just one of my paintings sold for $10,000, I'd be happy! I knew my art was just as good; if they could do it, so could I. This kind of thinking has brought me a long way. When I saw a local inventor succeed, I said, "She did it; I can invent too!" When I saw Robert Kiyosaki succeed in real estate, I said, "I can do it too!" It's the same with art! I can do it too.

WE ARE ALL CAPABLE; HOWEVER, UNLESS YOU BELIEVE YOU CAN DO IT, IT WON'T MANIFEST. It's time to start saying: "I can do it too!"

When I moved to my new home on the Big Island, I built an art studio, and it was a dream come true. I fell in love with the property because the energy was very peaceful and inspirational; it was a space for creation. I knew it was the perfect place to hold retreats and to start my art studio. I had several people offer to buy my first painting, so I knew I would need to find someone to make prints quickly. I had learned my lesson early on in elementary school when I was left with one portrait after I gave them all away instead of copying them; I'll keep the originals and only sell the prints. Of course, for the right price, the originals would definitely be for sale! Robert Nelson, Robert Wyland, and Peter Lik will continue to be inspirations for my art!

FIND A MENTOR AND ALLOW THEM TO INSPIRE YOU.

I have been having visions of opening a self-sustaining restaurant franchise. I am passionate about creating new business opportunities. I know there's opportunity and my vision is to partner with individuals who have the same passion. I desire to give back by mentoring small start-up businesses to help them follow their dreams.

EXERCISE:
DO SOMETHING FOR FREE!

Look closely, you're probably already doing it. Most people often do for free what they're passionate about; they don't care if they get paid because they love doing it. If there's not a job available for what you love to do, create one! Start small and get feedback if you require it. You can begin with family and friends, charging them little or nothing, then ask them to help you out with word-of-mouth advertising. Before you even know it, you may have a multitude of people requesting your services.

WINDOW OF OPPORTUNITY!

When you have a great idea for a product or business, you have to take action. Sometimes if you wait too long, you will miss the window of opportunity. In Shakespeare's "Julius Caesar," Brutus says, "There is a tide in the affairs of men, which, taken at the flood, leads on to fortune; omitted, all the voyage of their life is bound in shallows and in miseries." If you have a great idea for an invention and you don't strike while the iron is hot, I believe that idea will move on to someone else and then to the next, until finally, someone brings it to market. That's why, when you pass on an idea, you end up seeing it in the market in the future. When I was eight, I had a great idea to create a double eyelid for Asian eyes that would create a crease and make Asian eyes bigger. Then five years later, when I was thirteen years, I saw my idea selling in stores!

I DO THE OPPOSITE OF WHAT PEOPLE ARE DOING. If everyone is doing it, it's too late. When I started to invest in foreclosures, I could get them for real cheap. Then, two years later, everyone was buying them up, and the market went up. I stopped buying because the opportunity to get good deals had passed. When everyone starts doing the trendy thing, you can bet that it's going to be out of fashion real soon. You want to focus on buying when it's low and buying when others aren't!

ACCEPTANCE!

When I accept whatever life gives me, it keeps me grounded and I keep being inspired. My favorite line is, "Everything happens for a reason. Just wait; there's something great just around the corner." Each time something happens that I would perceive as bad, or when things don't go as I had planned, I get stressed. I want things to be a certain way. Since you can't change life, I had to just trust that it was for a reason.

MOMENTUM!

Whenever you have a burning desire, act on it, then take the next steps; make commitments. Sometimes, I jump into things because I know I desire it, then I realize I'm now committed. It helps me find solutions to make it happen. Sometimes, that works for me because I always find a way. It's better to just plunge forward than to not even take a step. This way, there's momentum and you can steer yourself in the right direction. I loved it when I did my first speech in California, a lot of my friends were disappointed that they couldn't come, so some suggested to me that I should give a speech in Honolulu after. At first, I was thinking, that's in two weeks; that's not enough time, but I booked it anyway and things fell into place. I then booked my Calgary speech for two weeks after, so I had to be focused and make that happen too! I used the momentum from my first speech to carry me on to the speech in Honolulu, and then on to my speech in Calgary. I rode the wave of momentum!

GET AHEAD!

The values of hard work and entrepreneurship were instilled in me at a young age. My mom and dad put me to work when I was eight, folding clothes. They started their own business in our basement with only $2,000 saved up. They bought their first sewing machine and my mom designed her own sportswear and exercise line of clothing at home.

She couldn't speak a lot of English then, but she still went out knocking door to door, getting purchase orders for her clothing line. I was very impressed—my mom and dad were new to the country and didn't know the language. They started with nothing and took a risk, going into business for themselves. With lots of hard work and determination, my parents turned their basement business into a multi-million dollar company with forty employees!

In 1986, spandex and leggings were popular, so my mom was designing and sewing jazz pants, tights, and fringed shirts. She ran her own marketing campaigns and met directly with buyers. People brought her samples, placed their orders, and she filled them!

There was never enough fabric at the stores my mom got her materials from. She decided to take action, and, using the name on the label, she was able to get in touch directly with the fabric supplier. When she first started placing orders direct with this supplier, she had to pay COD (cash on delivery).

My mom also sold her designs in malls and flea markets. Both my father and mother would sit there all day, hoping to sell her designs. Some days were discouraging for them. My mom recounted for me a story of a lady in the booth next to them who said, "If no one buys from you today, I will buy one or two." My mom remembers the support and kindness she felt, and those words really gave her hope.

At the end of that day, my mom had managed to sell $100 worth of product. The flea market was open only two days a week. Fortunately, the following week, there were some buyers from the city at the flea market. They found my mom's booth, liked her clothing, and asked if she could meet them the next day at their office. The very next day at the meeting, the new buyers gave my mom a large order for her products! My mom was so happy. Everything happens for a reason!

Instead of focusing her time at flea markets, my mom focused on finding the right fabric to fill her large order, as well as reaching out to other stores and shops for purchase orders. At the mall, she found a store called Body Things, which carried mostly exercise wear, and she secured a second order. She became very busy; one day, she sewed $2,000 worth of inventory all by herself. In the morning and afternoons, she

My family in the '80s.

did sales and marketing and secured more orders. Then she would cut and sew the clothes until midnight. She did that for a month.

My dad was working full time, so my mom hired some neighbors to help her sew. The three sisters from next door came and sewed in my mom's basement. She paid them in cash: $3.50 an hour. My mom was able to stop sewing and spend her time cutting and designing new patterns and sourcing fabrics. My dad had to quit his job to help out, and, at the age of seven, I also helped by folding clothes and trimming thread. I helped out in any way I could.

I learned how to work hard. I also got to sew some of my own designs. I made a collection of socks out of animal print and had fun sliding around the house in them. Thirty years later, I designed a line of sexy foot lingerie featuring animal prints!

Mai with celebrity Amanda Rigetti at the launch
of the Risque by Mai Lieu Lingerie line!

My older brother and I started sewing clothes while my younger brother took over the clothes folding and the thread trimming. It was a family business and we all desired for it to be a success.

My mom was such an inspiration to me. It's easy for me to look back at her business story and see the secret principles of success layered throughout.

When I looked around at my life, I realized that I was surrounded by very successful people. Most of them had financial freedom and they either owned a business or had investments in real estate. I had always desired to make a lot of money in business and then use that money to make real estate investments. Surrounding myself with people who were doing or had already done what I desired to do was essential to ensure my success!

If you desire to get ahead in this life, you have to start your own business. I hardly ever see people getting rich working for someone else!

My parents made lots of money in their business, but they also made a good deal of money in investments. This was a trend I needed to pay attention to! Since my business is considered high risk, I started looking for investments that were relatively stable. I love playing the CASHFLOW game; it really demonstrates how I operate when it comes to making money. I cannot wait to be at the point where I can be an artist just for the love of it, and not care if my passion brings in money. Funny thing about that: WHEN YOU START TO DO IT FOR THE LOVE OF IT, YOU START TO MAKE MONEY.

WHAT IS IT THAT YOU KNOW YOU'RE PUTTING OFF, WHAT ARE YOU GOING TO DO TODAY THAT WILL FURTHER YOUR DREAM?

Charles Dederich of Synanon once said, "Today is the first day of the rest of your life."

WHAT CAN YOU DO TODAY THAT WILL CHANGE YOUR LIFE?

Just take the first step and keep growing and then take the next step, any step, even if it's small.

LEGACY!

I desire to leave a legacy through my products. My inventions led me to write this book and become an inspirational speaker so that I could share my story and inspire millions to follow their dreams. Each step led to the next. I never would have thought all this could happen. This is why it's so important to just take one step, any step; it will lead you to something great! You never know, it may change your life. By taking a step and taking a risk, I am living the life of my dreams.

When I took those first steps, and followed my passion in hair and martial arts, I never thought it would lead me to living in China, then later living in Hawaii and becoming an inventor. I have already created four inventions, and I have so many great ideas; I know there will be many more to come.

My second invention: CreaNails! (Photo by Tung Bui)

When I pass away, my products will continue to help people. I love that I am making a difference in the world with my products.

What idea do you have that could change the world? JUST GO FOR IT. I did it; so can you!

I see the value of doing a business plan, as well as a life plan. I have created a Master Life Plan for myself. I plan out everything I desire to accomplish in a year. I set all my intentions; then I break down my goals, and I schedule tasks that will need to be completed each month to achieve my plan. Since nothing ever goes exactly as planned, I simply adjust the plan as I go. When I plan things, they happen.

EXERCISE:
MASTER LIFE PLAN

1 YEAR PLAN
Write out the things you desire to manifest in the first year in the categories below. When you are clear and plan ahead, the easier it is to manifest the life of your dreams.

1. Work or Business
   Examples:
   a. Increase sales by 30%
   b. Focus on Marketing
   c. Launch Kickstarter Campaign
   d. Launch New Product
   e. Publish Book
2. Health and fitness
3. Relationship
4. Spiritual

Now write it out like it has already happened:
   Example:
   a. I am so grateful now that I am living the life of my dreams, creating financial liberty and loving my relationships.

5 YEAR PLAN

Write a sentence, or paragraph, describing what you desire to achieve in the next 5 years in each category. Remember, don't think about how or if you can do it, just write down what you desire. Think of it like a winning ticket and you can create whatever you desire.

Example details:
   Examples:
   a. Build a family
   b. Build my dream home
   c. Have five more Vacation rentals
   d. Launch three more new products
   e. Enter a 5K marathon

10 YEAR PLAN

Write a paragraph that includes what you desire in 10 years, just have fun and dream big! Anything is possible.

3 MONTH ACTION PLAN

MONTH 1

Break your plan down to each month and week. Set goals of what you would like to achieve in each week. Make sure you keep it balanced in each category.

Week 1

Example

a. Business Goal: increase sales; action: Contact three new bloggers & send them samples for review.
b. Fitness Goals: Prepare meals; Monday and Wed work out.
c. Relationship Goals: Date night once a week and two acts of love.
d. Spiritual Goal: Meditate three times this week.

Week 2

Week 3

Week 4

MONTH 2

MONTH 3

When you finish each month, continue and add on another month. This way, you will always have three months planned out. Do a whole year and then update it as you go. You might manifest your goals faster, so be prepared to revise as necessary! Stay clear and focused; most important, take action.

KEEP SETTING GOALS!

Once I was successful, I stopped planning and then I stopped growing. No matter where you are in your life, you must continue to set goals so you will continue to grow. My goal setting worked in the past, so why not do it again? A quick ninety days of affirmation and I was back on track! You've got to keep setting goals!

In my business, I set yearly, monthly, and weekly goals. As my business grows, I find it very supportive to set daily goals. I usually set them the day before so that I'm in a centered space when I start my day. When I hear my procrastinator voice trying to talk me out of my task list, it's easier to identify it as the voice of ego. I stay clear and on purpose because I already know what I desire.

It's important to set goals. It helps you grow and take risks. When you set goals, you have a direction, and you head toward your goal with focus. Mark Victor Hansen wrote, "What you think about comes about." And Thomas Wilhite wrote, "To think is to create. What the mind can conceive, you can achieve."

It's all so true. When I hear these words over and over, I believe them. It's easy to create results and then stop. If it works, why not continue to do it again? CONTINUE TO CHALLENGE YOURSELF THROUGH GOAL SETTING. When you set goals, make sure you set goals with an element of risk, and you have to believe that it is possible. Before I set a goal (like creating twenty-nine million in sales), I make sure it's risky and it's something I desire and can really see happening. My final check was: Would I bet on it? I asked myself, "Would I bet $10,000 on achieving my goal?" If I wouldn't bet on it, then I really didn't believe it would happen.

Make sure you have all three:
1. Is it a risk you desire?
2. Can you see it?
3. Would you bet on it?

SUCCESSFUL PEOPLE PLAN!

One of the reasons why I'm able to accomplish so much is because I plan ahead. I noticed when I would make plans to go surfing with my girlfriends, it happens. If I've registered for a class, I always make time for it, especially if it cost me money. I would rearrange my day, even if it wasn't the most important thing. When I travel, I have everything planned ahead of time. That way, I get everything I desire done. If I don't plan, I end up doing what others want me to do, which is okay if it's something I desire to be doing. But what if it's not? When I have a plan, it makes it clearer for me to stay focused on what I love to do. It's more likely to happen because I carve out the time to do it!

INVEST IN PERSONAL DEVELOPMENT.

In business, it's just as important to continue investing in your personal development as it is to plan and set goals. It's like the gym; you can buy the membership, but if you don't go and lift those weights, you won't earn those muscles. If you stop using your muscles, they disappear.

The first three years of my business, I was on fire. I had been introduced to the power of my mind. I practiced it, applied it, and created amazing results. Once my business was doing well, I got comfortable and thought I'd take a break. That was dangerous because there's no such thing as stability. I stopped using the concepts, I stopped visualizing and affirming, and my muscles got weak. When challenges came, the fears and self-doubt came back too.

Just keep growing. As you reach milestones, set new goals and make new dream boards. IF THE TOOLS WORK, KEEP USING THEM.

When I was young, we were poor. The other kids teased us, and I was embarrassed. Experiences like that fueled me towards financial freedom.

Meanwhile, in the clothing business, my mom had begun working with a wholesaler who sold t-shirts, and she had greatly expanded her product line to support the demand from her clients. With the popularity of fleece in 1987 to 1988, she landed some pretty big accounts. The economy was growing and the 1988 Olympics in Calgary brought her some great business. She supplied them with T-shirts, tank tops, fleece shirts, and hockey jerseys. Orders for the Olympics were 10,000 to 50,000 pieces at a time!

Eight months later, the business had grown so much they moved the business to a warehouse, bought more sewing machines, and hired over twenty employees! Running the business at home, my mom made a decent amount of money, but with the warehouse and employees, she made $5,000 a day! There was no room to put the fabric, so they had to move again. More businesses found her, and business boomed.

She made over $300,000 net per year from 1989-1990. In 1992, my parents bought their dream home, a commercial building for the clothing business, and even a restaurant business. Within twelve years, we went from living in the basement of my uncle's house with my grandparents to buying our dream home.

The family clothing business grew and expanded quickly!

In elementary school, my lunch consisted of one piece of toast. But when I was eighteen, my father bought me a brand new red Honda Del Sol sports car. I cherished it and kept it in mint condition. My father worked hard and gave his family everything he had, while he drove a beat-up old Toyota Tercel that was used for restaurant deliveries. He desired the best for all of us. I was always grateful for my parents and I knew that one day, I would be taking care of them.

My mom in action, cutting out one of her designs in the warehouse.

In 1992, the introduction of the Free Trade Agreement caused a slump for the manufacturing business. It was hard to compete with China's cheap prices and labor. Yet, my mom was still able to keep the company running, and the restaurant made money to balance things. In the end, my family sold the business along with the commercial building, and increased their wealth, and their investments.

I feel like I am following in my parents' footsteps. Even when my mom would sell clothes at the flea market, I had the entrepreneurial spirit. I would buy rubber bracelets at the flea market in a pack of ten for only a dollar. At the mall, they were selling them for a dollar each! I

ACHIEVE FINANCIAL LIBERTY

was only eight years old, but I knew this was a good return on invest-ment. Everyone at school had about twenty of them on their wrists because those rubber bracelets were the "in" thing, so I decided to buy the packs at the flea market, and sell them for a profit to the students at school. Each time I sold out of bracelets, I would use the profit to buy more bracelets. I was running a side business while I worked for my mom folding clothes!

At nine years old, I started a club called "The Dynamite Girls" with all the popular girls. We all wore uniforms made from my mom's de-signs with the stylish fringe shirts and purple and black striped tights. I even designed a logo that had "The Dynamite Girls" in a Z-formation and silk-screened it to the shirts. I made it popular to wear the tights my mom designed, and everyone wanted to be in the club and buy them. I desired to help my mom any way I could and I was good at selling!

Later, at 19, I noticed my mom had a bunch of clothes in storage. They were returns, overstock, or clothes with minor defects. I thought, why not sell them at a discounted price? They were just sitting in stor-age, taking up space. I decided to make signs and asked the gas stations if I could put up a sign. Back then it was easy to do that kind a thing. The signs I made said, "New Clothing Sale! T-shirts $3.00" and the location and date. I posted them on the poles at intersections, at a popular gas station, at stop signs, etc. I made sure there were signs everywhere. I put up racks and racks of clothing on the side of the street and a big sign next to the Van that read, "Sportswear Sale." I told people I was rais-ing money for my university tuition. I knew it would be more fun to have my friend working with me, plus we could sell a lot more if there were two of us. I paid her an hourly rate of $10 an hour, which was very good at the time, plus I paid her 10% commission. It was the most money she'd made in her life!

The sale was a big hit. Crowds of people came and they bought piles and piles of clothes! My bargaining skills got really good. We brought in over a thousand dollars that day, and my mom said I could just keep it all, since I had taken the initiative, and the clothing had just been sitting in storage. I decided to have a sale the next weekend too! People kept asking if I would be back.

I learned so much from this experience; the knowledge and experience I gained was better than anything I could learn at university. I learned how to sell, market, and negotiate!

I had "sportswear" sales for two summers, and, when traffic slowed, I moved my sale location to a different gas station near my parents' restaurant. There was more traffic, and I had already sold to all the potential customers at the old location. I was making so much money, my brothers were getting jealous, and I had to give them a commission because they thought it wasn't fair. No one thought I would sell so much. The first year, the police came by and asked us what we were doing, but they didn't say anything, and let us continue. However, by the third year, they told me I needed a license. So I got one. But even with a license, the following year, the police shut us down. They said it was illegal to sell on the side of the street out of a van. Yes it was, when I think about it, but it was a pretty cool experience.

I did it for four years and it gave me confidence, empowering me to try things and not be afraid. It was my first summer business. Even when people said I wasn't going to sell anything, or it wouldn't work, I just tried anyway, and I was successful. Sometimes you just have to do it anyway.

CHAPTER 7

THE BIGGER
THE CHALLENGE,
THE BIGGER THE GROWTH

Growth demands a temporary surrender of security.
—*Gail Sheehy*

When I speak, I talk about my many successes, but I also share my challenges because I want people to know that it's okay to have obstacles and fears and doubts; they don't mean you can't succeed! People will ask, "Mai, you always seem so grounded; do you have any challenges, any fears?" I say, "Yes, and they're always there, but I handle them a lot differently. I don't let them hold me back."

Things were really humming along in my life. And then it happened. I saw a notification from Google, and I clicked on a link that took me to a page with a new product; a knockoff of the CreaClip. I was furious! How could they do that? They had completely copied my product and were now selling it. My sales dropped by 30% that month and continued to decline to 50%. I started to freak out. I was in panic mode; I had so many negative voices telling me things were not going to be okay and I was asking doubtful questions. "What are you going to do? How are you going to keep your company running when sales are dropping so much? What if it keeps going down to nothing? You are not going to be okay." I was stressed and worried. I even called my CPA and let him go because I was worried I couldn't pay him next month if things were going to go in this direction. I didn't know how I was going to pay for my expenses. I was getting credit card bills with unpaid balances of $20,000 and my savings were going down and down. I always kept a certain amount in the bank, and it made me feel safe and it had gone down past my safety zone. I felt vulnerable, and worried that things were not going to be okay.

I directed my attention and focused on all the things I was grateful for, and it helped me be in a better state for a while. But as soon as another credit card bill came in, the fear and worry would come back. It was like I was bipolar. One moment I was okay, and then the next, I was thinking things were falling apart and fearing the future. I used all the tools I had to shift out of it. I started to write down all the benefits of what's happening. That helped for a while, but as I watched my bank account go down, it wasn't enough to make it last. Then, I remembered:

THERE'S ALWAYS A SOLUTION TO EVERY OBSTACLE.

When you attend PSI seminars, you are automatically given the opportunity to return for another round of seminars as a way to refresh, and it's free. So I did it. In the early years of my business, I would attend a seminar anytime I had a challenge, and after a weekend of thinking positively and being surrounded with positive energy, I left feeling empowered. When my business was doing well, I volunteered and gave back to the community that had supported me by becoming a session group leader. This time, I was going back as a student again; I needed to break through my challenges.

Fortunately for me, the instructor, Paul Thede, was also an inventor. He invented a part for motorcycle suspension. He also held the world record for the fastest man on the electric motorcycle! I asked Paul if others copied his invention. He said, "Yes, and they are selling it for so cheap." I asked, "What do you do?" He said. "Mine's the best." I thought the same; mine is the best.

Instead of focusing on the knockoffs, I needed to focus on developing new products. I got into solution mode. I made a goal to increase sales. During those months of challenges, I came up with another invention, CreaLash! The motivation of a new product idea fueled me and I started developing it right away. I became proactive and created packages that included the CreaClip and a pair of scissors. I also created packaging to market CreaClip Pet for cutting your dog's or horse's hair. My inspiration for the CreaClip Pet came directly from my customers! One wrote "I love the CreaClip; I even used it on my Yorkie. I was able to give her the perfect trim. Thank you for inventing this." Another customer thanked me via email; she used the CreaClip on her horse to cut the mane and it gave the perfect straight cut. So I created a package for Pets!

Keep focusing on developing new products!

*The CreaClip Pet was inspired by feedback
from my customers.* (photo by Chris Hirata)

With so many projects in the works, I knew one of them had to hit it big. Like my mom always said, "when you cut off a tree, more branches grow from the sides." That's how I felt, like I was growing back stronger and in different ways. I felt empowered and prepared.

Thankfully, I had created multiple streams of income. When the sales in my business went down, my long-term rentals still paid for all my expenses. While my savings were decreasing, I had to shift my attention and see where my money was, instead of where it wasn't. Instead of perceiving the money as being lost, I chose to believe that it was just being stored in a different location than my bank account. The real estate investments were also my savings; they just weren't as liquid. I wasn't really missing anything; nothing was really lost. I paid cash for the properties, so I could pull out my capital and leverage it with a mortgage whenever I desired to! My investments in real estate were better used there than sitting in the bank; those properties were making me money while I slept.

When you have a business, cash flow is always a tricky thing to balance, but I learned. I started to shift my thinking from "not having enough" to "there's nothing wrong" and "everything is okay."

I ACHIEVE MY DREAM
OF BECOMING AN INSPIRATIONAL SPEAKER!

Winning the Principia Conference Speaking Competition was really exciting. By the time I found out about the competition, it had been running for two weeks already. I hurriedly shot my video, spent all night editing it, posted it to Facebook, and then messaged my friends to vote for me.

I have over 2,000 friends on Facebook, and, that week, I messaged every one of them personally. I was shocked by the amount of support I received.

I created a following from this competition; friends of friends started adding me, and they were voting for me each day. I was attracting like-minded people who followed their dreams; entrepreneurs and people who believed in transformation.

It was the first time I led so many people. I was inspiring people through my actions and inspirational story, but this time I was leading a group of people with the same purpose, and I got to experience the power of collectiveness.

WHEN EVERYONE IS THINKING AND ENVISIONING
THE SAME GOAL AND MOVING TOWARD THE SAME PURPOSE,
IT IS EASIER TO MANIFEST.

Imagine the power of thousands putting out the same intention. I was leading each day by 100-200 votes; I knew we'd win the competition and I was going to be a featured speaker.

As the deadline for the competition approached, they decided to extend it for three more days and have round two. As a business, it made sense to keep it going as a great social media marketing tool, but it didn't seem fair to me. Our team fought hard for this win; now, I felt ripped off. I gave it my all, and I felt like I could not keep going for three more days. I wanted to give up.

My husband was torn to see me so crushed. He knew it meant a lot to me. And he was ready to fight for me. My family and friends were also upset. Aline from our Women Power Group said, "Mai, you can't give up; you can't stop this, even if you wanted to. Look, they had reset the number of votes and you already have seventy votes; people are still continuing to vote for you." People were putting negative comments about the reset on Facebook, and I was touched by how people were willing to fight for me and stand up for me. I also knew I was leading them in a negative direction.

I had to shift out of feeling like a victim; I knew being in that state was not going to create the results I desired. I got really clear about my purpose for becoming an inspirational speaker. "Why, Mai? Why do you desire so badly to be on that stage?" I asked myself. The answer: I desired to share my message and inspire the world. If I quit now, I would probably stop and never look back. I was not going to let my team down. I was going to win so they could be inspired and hear my message and help other people. When my purpose is focused on others, when it's about contributing to the world, I don't let anything get in the way. It's not about me anymore; it's about inspiring the world.

I sent out a mass message and channeled my team's energy in a more positive direction. I showed them a different perspective, and, to add compassion, I said, "This is the first time they are having this Facebook competition; they are doing their best. Let's focus our energy on getting more votes and finishing what we started!" I couldn't believe how I was able to shift people's energy and lead them in a positive direction.

WE ARE ALWAYS LEADING PEOPLE BY OUR ACTIONS WHETHER IT'S POSITIVE OR NEGATIVE.

This was such a great opportunity for me to see how I was as a leader. In the second round, my team stepped up. They reached out to all their friends and got more votes; we became stronger as a team. It was a learning experience for all of us. It brought me closer to my husband, my friends, my family, and everyone who voted for me.

On the last day of voting, I knew we had won, and at that point, it didn't matter if I was chosen to be a speaker or not. I planned to throw a party for all the people who voted for me, with food and games, to celebrate because we had won in so many ways. I was grateful for the growth I had experienced. I experienced what it felt like not to give up when physically, mentally, and emotionally, I couldn't move forward.

When they announced the results, there were two winners, exactly what I had desired, and we would share the stage! I had the most combined votes overall, so I was chosen to be the speaker from round 1. Matt had the most votes in the second round, and he was also going to speak!

PSI Seminars acknowledged their mistake and I had already come to a place of acceptance.

WE ARE NOT PERFECT AND WE WILL CONTINUE TO MAKE MISTAKES. ALL WE CAN DO IS TRY OUR BEST AND LEARN FROM OUR EXPERIENCES.

Nothing is a failure if you learn from it. I chose to see the benefit, which allowed me to move forward; I do that with every challenge. I trust that it's happening for a reason and it's perfect just the way it is. I actually thanked the person who extended the Facebook competition; I grew so much out of it. My win was extremely fulfilling. I joked that next year, they should mess the competition up on purpose so we can be challenged. WHEN THERE'S A CHALLENGE, TRUST THAT IT'S FOR A REASON, AND THERE'S SOMETHING GREAT FOR YOU AROUND THE CORNER!

I found out that I was speaking at the end of the conference. That was not good. I had the whole week to be nervous! I just wanted to do it right away so I could relax. I spoke with Paul Thede, and he gave me some coaching. He'd been speaking for years, and he told me to just go out there and be you; it's okay to mess up. What a great environment for me to be in for my first time speaking on stage. I was surrounded by positive-thinking people, friends who support me; and I spoke to a group of industry leaders who were open and loving.

The first day, Michael Beckwith was on, and he said something that really shifted me out of being in fear. He said, "What is your purpose? My purpose is to inspire and share my message. That's it. That's all I have to do, go on stage and just share. It doesn't matter if I'm not perfect. It doesn't matter how I do it. Just be authentic."

The week went by real fast, listening to Bob Proctor, Mike Dooly, and Marshal Thurber. I learned so much, and what an honor it was to share the same stage. These were the inspirational speakers I had learned from and looked up to, and I got to be in the VIP sitting area with them, preparing to go on stage!

The speaker line-up for the Principia 2013 Conference. Saturday at 9:30!

Kathy, who was the advanced instructor for PSI seminars, coached me the night before and helped me refine my speech. I was so grateful to have her support. I texted her before I went to bed and told her I was ready and I was going to rock it.

In the VIP section, Rob Rohe, another advanced instructor, was holding my hand the whole thirty minutes before I had to go on stage. It allowed me to stay present and not allow the fear to get in my head. I felt so much love and support, and before I knew it, they were announcing me: "Everyone, please welcome Mai Lieu!"

I had asked them to play my song while I walked on stage, *Roar* by Katy Perry. My mother in-law heard it on the radio and said it reminded her of me.

ROAR
You held me down, but I got up…!
Already brushing off the dust
You hear my voice, you hear that sound
Like thunder gonna shake the ground
You held me down, but I got up ....
I've got the eye of the tiger, a fighter, dancing through the fire
'Cause I am a champion and you're gonna hear me roar!

It was the perfect song for my opening. It brings tears to my eyes each time I hear it. It was like I was walking into the ring! The moment I stepped on the stage, I was on, I was present, and things just flowed. I was in the zone again! I joked about how they gave Bob Proctor a clock to keep time while speaking, but where was mine.

The audience was laughing and crying. I took them on a roller coaster, sharing my ups and downs. I asked them what was holding them back. I told them that their idea and their dreams could one day change the world. I inspired them to take action now… I inspired them to take that next step!

Thirty minutes went by fast and I had so much fun on stage. I was on fire; I was in the red zone. When I got off the stage, people rushed up to congratulate me and tell me how amazing I had been; how I'd said the perfect thing, right when they needed to hear it.

One gentleman, also from Calgary, said, "Mai, I was confused about which business to start and what direction to take and you said "just take the next step, any step, and it will lead to the next." That's what I'm going to do, just one step, because I've been stuck for a long time."

I posted my speech on Youtube, and the feedback I received was amazing. My cousin called me and said, "Mai, I loved your speech, it was so amazing. I wanted to share with you that I got an interior design contract with Facebook! What a big win!"

She visited me in Hawaii earlier that year. She desired to go on a retreat and it hadn't worked out, so I thought I'd give her a private retreat of her own on my property. We did coaching and exercises to help her break through her thinking, plus we surfed and hiked. We meditated and ate healthy. Imagine doing that every day!

After one week, she broke through her fears and was excited; she decided to move and commit to her dream of starting her own business venture in San Francisco. For weeks after she went home, she would call me and say, "Mai, how am I going to do this? I'm so afraid." I would say, "Good, FEAR IS A SIGN YOU ARE GOING IN THE RIGHT DIRECTION." She'd be okay for a while, but then, weeks later, she'd be afraid again and say, "Mai, I'm running out of money." I reassured her everything was okay and that there was a reason she was there.

Now, she not only landed a contract, it was with a huge company, Facebook! Just take the next step!

I get real excited when I see people following their passions and creating success. So many people have great ideas but their fears hold them back. Once you overcome your obstacles, there will be no stopping you! Here's the YouTube video link of the 40th Principia speech: https://www.youtube.com/watch?v=gfOo5kSLDwM

EXERCISE:
CHALLENGE YOURSELF

Think of something you're afraid of doing, like public speaking or diving off the high diving board, or scuba diving. Make a resolution to do it and set it in motion. Join a Toastmaster's club or sign up for diving lessons. Pay attention to your thoughts during the lead up to your icebreaker speech, or your first high dive or deep dive. What is your negative voice telling you? Is it telling you to quit before you humiliate or hurt yourself? Ignore it and face the challenge. Break the ice and take the plunge.

We need to be "challenged" in our lives in order to grow. One cannot exist without the other. When there is challenge, you get to think outside the box and come up with solutions. The word "challenge" used to seem like a bad thing, but now, I honestly believe it is necessary to grow as an individual as well as an entrepreneur.

Before the sales started coming in, I had worked hard for years with no pay. I ran out of investment funds and thought that if something didn't pan out, I would have to move back to Canada and live with my mom. It is funny now when I write it, but I really did have a negative voice that would pop up to remind me that I was too afraid or that I couldn't do it. The negative voice sounded so believable at first; however, each time I proved it wrong. I would hear the voice, but still face the challenge and take one more step.

CHALLENGES MAKE YOU STRONGER!

Going into this business, experts told me upfront that when I became successful, others would copy me, so it was kind of a compliment. As Charles Caleb Colton wrote, "Imitation is the sincerest form of flattery." But I know it doesn't feel good when you think of it as losing potential sales. However, you have a choice. You can think of it as loss, or you can think of it as gain. New inventions translate into more money, so nothing is really lost and something is gained! LEARN FROM CHALLENGES, SO THERE'S NO SUCH THING AS FAILURE!

Challenges always happen; it's the universe's way of testing how committed you are. Obstacles were put in my path, over and over, and I grew from them. When things didn't work out in one direction, I would just shift the sail and go in a different direction. I would learn from every experience. When I saw myself going down a hole with no cheese, I would stop, call it a loss and not invest any more money.

YOU'VE GOT TO KNOW WHEN TO STOP.

I know when to stop putting time and money in a project. When my first commercials didn't work, I didn't give up. I hired another marketing company, but we never finished the media testing because of a lawsuit. I took this as a sign that I was not heading in the right direction. I changed my direction and focused on growing my following on YouTube.

I didn't beat myself up; I just learned from it and took the next step. IF YOU LEARN FROM EVERY EXPERIENCE, NOTHING

CAN BE BAD. I know that the universe balances everything, and when I focus on the positive not just the negative, I feel much better. ENERGY IS NOT WASTED ON THE PAST BUT INVESTED ON WHAT'S NEXT!

When people struggle, they tend to go into a cave. I do the same. I don't desire to let people know that I am struggling. But then I realize that it's so much easier to ask for support. I call my friends and family, and they help me see things through a different perspective. We all go through cycles of ups and downs, but if you never give up, you are always growing. There are times when I'm in the hole so deep I really don't know how I'm going to get out. That's when the voice whispers, "See, this is the end of your dream. Now you get to go back to Canada and live with your mom." It seems so real, but each time, I don't give up. I will not believe that voice!

There will always be ups and downs, and the more success you create, the larger those ups and downs can be. They go from $2,000 problems to $20,000 problems to $2-million-dollar problems. No matter how much money you make, the thought processes are always there. I still have to consciously choose not to let my voices hold me back, and it has gotten easier.

Now, I look for challenges so that I can grow! When I get thrown down by a challenge, I get back up, and I feel much stronger. Another mentor of mine, Marshall Thurber, has a teaching similar to my mom's. He terms this concept *Go-Hydra*, and it's based on a Greek myth; when you cut a Lernaean Hydra's head off, two grow back; if you cut the two, four grow back; and so on. Hearing this philosophy reconfirmed that I was planning to Go-Hydra. I was stronger than ever with four heads! I went from fearing the future to being excited about what's coming next!

KNOCKOFFS!

I knew, going into my business, that once my product was a success, others would create knockoffs of my product. I was determined to stay one step ahead and brand myself as the original. I was also prepared to fight.

132

I spent thousands of dollars on attorney fees to get my competition removed. I love Ebay and Amazon; they removed them right away. Ebay removed them in five minutes!

Now, I am experiencing the other side of the proverbial Lernaean Hydra coin. When you cut off the head of an imitator, two more heads grow. But, I was also growing four heads.

The competition did not play fair. They were using my photos and videos on their sites! I had created a special package for Japan, and they were using the exact packaging, and even using our old company name! The saddest part? People buy it, not knowing it's a low-quality knockoff.

The pain of business and inventing! Look at Louis Vuitton, there are so many knockoffs. Yes, some people buy the knockoffs, but most desire the original. I have customers who write to me to make sure we are the original before they buy it.

I put a lot of money into stopping the knockoffs, but then I chose to enforce what I could for now and put most of my energy into developing products. I could fight and have the "there's not enough" philosophy, or I could think about abundance and create more. I won't give up.

I am inspired to keep taking the next step by focusing on the reasons I started my business. Why did I desire to invent the CreaClip? It was to help families who couldn't afford haircuts to have beautiful hair also. It's the same with my other products, I love that it brings joy to children when they learn how to paint their own nails with CreaNails. That's the reason. I keep moving forward, I keep my vision clear, and I keep inventing new products.

If I had let the knockoffs get me down, I wouldn't have come up with my new products. It's not about the money; it's about making a difference in the world through my products.

I've inspired so many people just by following my own dreams. It inspired them to also do the same, and if I give up, I would be doing a disservice to them. Plus, I would never give up on myself. I am successful because I never give up and I always take the next step.

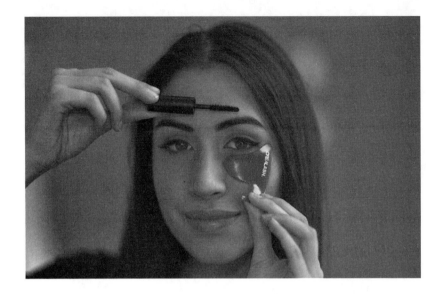

The CreaLash product came to me as the result of a challenge I was presented with. (Photo by Tung Bui)

EVERYTHING HAPPENS FOR A REASON.

I love what I do; I get to invent products! When I was trying to get my product on a shopping channel; I tried super hard and I invested money to fly there, but it didn't work out. Instead of thinking I had failed, I took it as a sign that I was not going in the right direction and I stayed open to opportunities, which lead me to HSN! When things don't happen the way you desire them, just trust there's a better way. The same thing happened to another inventor, Walt Disney. He went to New York to renew his contract for the Oswald the Rabbit cartoon. He didn't reach a deal; they wanted to steal his creation. But instead of feeling discouraged, he created a new cartoon character on the train ride back to Los Angeles, Mickey Mouse. And the rest is history.

What I noticed about challenges was that I would only see what was happening at the moment. If sales happened to be going down, I would take that as a bad sign, rather than just as a tiny downturn in a larger and longer cycle of positive growth.

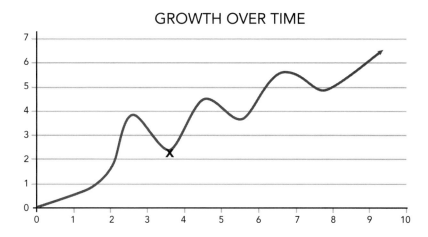

Stay focused on the big picture in your business growth.
Ups and downs are part of the game.

In the beginning, my business sales grew and ballooned dramatically after I sold out on HSN! A year later, my sales fell dramatically after signing an exclusive deal with an infomercial company. My sales went down, but they never went below the level they were at when I first started selling.

I came up with solutions to market my product and the sales went back up again, and I broke my highest sales record. I was always growing, so my lows were never lower than my lowest and my highs were higher than the previous highs! I began to see the big picture of a long-term growth cycle. I got excited thinking about all the sales I was going to make in the future! I went from thinking that a downturn in sales was bad to thinking it was the part of the cycle before a higher uptick in sales!

As the poet Shelley wrote, "If Winter comes, can Spring be far behind?" Each winter, the fruit tree starts off bare and barren, but each spring and summer, it produces leaves, blossoms, and fruit, and over the years, it keeps growing. If you never give up, you'll always grow! Trust that everything happens for a reason.

THERE IS SOMETHING GREAT AROUND THE CORNER.

When knockoffs of my product caused a drop in my sales, I learned a few things about how to deal with the stress. My mentor and teacher, Cheri Huber, taught me a few things that helped me to stay focused, and I'd like to share them with you.

EXERCISE:
MAKE RECORDINGS THAT YOU LISTEN TO DAILY:

First thing in the morning, listen to a recording that has reassurances and affirmations and starts you off on a positive note.

EXERCISE:
MEDITATE

Set aside time to meditate during the week. Start with small amounts of time at first and build from there. It's not compassionate when you make it a requirement. Repeat reassuring words to yourself so that solutions will come to you easily. Say, "I am enough, I am capable, everything is okay, the universe is on my side, there's something great around the corner, just trust and let go." Just keep adding reassuring affirmations, whatever makes you feel like you can relax.

EXERCISE:
BUILD A SUPPORT GROUP

Find friends who won't let you give up. Don't think you're just too busy to ask for support! Don't try to do everything yourself. When you ask for support, everything is so much easier. One of the top reasons I have created so much success is my reliance on the support system I have created.

One day (mid-challenge), I came up with a very creative haircut and posted it on YouTube. It exploded with hits! This encouraged me to do more of the same; Now, I have new ideas for videos about how to use CreaProducts. I have so much in place that I just know it's all going to come together like small waves coming together to produce a swell, and, like a surfer, I'll be riding my biggest high.

I am always growing, so my graph just keeps going up and up. Now, I trust that it's all part of the roller coaster ride, up and down, up and down, but over time, the sales go up. I no longer freak out when sales are going down; I can enjoy the ride. Giving up is not even an option!

My life coach, David, says, "Every day is a win, if you look at it that way." Even if you don't reach your goal, you have already won. That's right. When you enjoy the journey, it really doesn't matter if you achieve the goal or not. Just learn and enjoy! I have grown so much already, and I am excited for more!

As the Swedish pop group Abba sings, "Money, money, money, must be funny in a rich man's world." We all have a responsibility to learn about budgeting and saving money. As I've grown my businesses, I've had to be very aware of money, and get good at budgeting; there's a tendency to spend more when you make more, which is fine, as long as you aren't spending more than you're making! It's always good to have savings, just in case there's an emergency.

EXERCISE:

APPLYING SUCCESS TO OTHER AREAS

You have already created success in your life. Look back on those successes, write them down and give yourself a pat on the back. Now, think back to those times when you "nailed it." How did you do it? How did you feel? Were you in the zone? Did you plan things in a special way? Was it something you were passionate about? Discover the principles that worked for you and apply those same principles now! We're all successful in areas we value most. Whatever is most important to us, we're most disciplined at.

For example, in my business, when something didn't go as planned, I knew there was a reason, and I always found a solution. That's how I achieved success in my business.

I realized that I could apply the same thought process to my relationship with my husband. When our relationship started to get tough, I immediately worried, "Maybe he's not the one; maybe there's someone better out there for me." I realized I had followed this same pattern of thinking before I got married and I was dating; when things got hard, I would just find someone else, only to find out that he wasn't the one either! I knew I had to change my thinking.

So I asked a question: "What would I do if this relationship were my business?" When things get tough in my business, I always find a solution; I don't give up! I found my solution, and my husband and I are closer than ever.

THERE'S SOMETHING GOOD IN EVERY EXPERIENCE.

Coming to Canada when I was four was so exciting! There were a lot of great things about moving, yet, like everything in life, there were some challenges, too. Canada is a multicultural country, and most people we met were very nice and accepting, but as with any country, there are people who are just mean. One particular story stands out for me.

My brothers and I walked home from the bus stop after school, and there was one house we hated having to walk past. There was a small group of kids at the house on the corner who would say some pretty mean things to us each day as we passed by. I remember them singing the famous "Me Chinese, me no dumb" song. Kids always find ways to make fun of other kids.

I was intimidated at first; I felt like I needed to fit in and I tried to learn English as fast as I could so I would "blend in." I remember coming home after my first day of school and I started just rambling words I'd made up, pretending I knew how to speak English. I even fooled my mom for a while. She was so impressed that after just one day, I could speak English. I fooled her for a week, until the day she asked me to translate. I had to tell her I was just making it up.

It was a challenging time, learning a new language and going to ESL classes. Kids looked at me like I was an outsider. But I adapted fast. This taught me to be a strong and persistent child. I had to be flexible, and I found solutions for everything because I knew I had to make it work. Our family went through a lot to get to Canada and we were determined, together, to make a new life.

The other day, I was out walking and saw a swing set. It brought back a memory I haven't even thought of for over thirty-five years. When I was five, our sponsors and some other people from church generously donated a swing set to us. I was so happy to play on it! Then, in the middle of the night, some kids took the swing set and put it in the street. My parents had to run out and move it back before it got run over.

I felt so vulnerable and scared. It's funny how these memories are still in my mind, even after thirty years. There was a time when I perceived that experience as bad and negative. Now, I see the benefit I received from this experience, and that has removed any negative energy. Something good always comes out of every experience!

You can perceive an experience as good or bad; it's up to you. One day, I saw a man run into a sign because it was hanging too low; he got really mad and started swearing. A second man came by and did the same thing; he hit himself really hard on that sign, but he just laughed. Same experience, different reaction.

WE CREATE OUR OWN EXPERIENCE. WHY NOT CREATE A GREAT ONE!

People often tell me to not do things because they themselves had experienced something bad. Sometimes, I take their advice, but other times, if it's something I feel strongly about, I do it anyway because I know I create my own experience! Everyone is different, and each situation is unique. They may have had a bad experience with someone they worked with or didn't like something. That does not mean I will have the same experience; I'm not them. Ethan used to say, "I don't like spaghetti," and I would say, "That's because you never had mine!" BE OPEN!

WHAT YOU GIVE IS WHAT YOU GET BACK.

I really believe this. The more I give unconditionally, the more I get back. The universe always finds a way to give you more. However, it goes both ways. If I'm frustrated, defensive, or angry when I speak to my husband, I get that same energy back.

The same principle applies to positive energy! If I respond with a light, funny remark, the other person's face changes, and they too are pleasant to be with. I notice this everywhere I go. When people are angry and mad, I just laugh, joke, and make light of the situation. They immediately change and laugh with me. Sometimes, people don't even know what they are laughing about, but because I'm laughing, they laugh too!

The energy we put out is very contagious. We have the power to bring out any feeling we choose. What do you choose? I feel so empowered when someone is mad and they say mean things to try and make me mad too, and I stay calm and peaceful. I don't give my power away! My energy attracts people!

FIND BALANCE

*I believe that being successful means having a balance
of success stories across the many areas of your life.
You can't truly be considered successful in your business
life if your home life is in shambles.*
—Zig Ziglar

I have seen a lot of successful business owners who make a ton of money, but they don't have solid relationships, or they are overweight, out of shape, and they don't take time to enjoy their hobbies or travel. I have also seen people who have amazing relationships, but they struggle when it comes to their careers or their business. I believe you can have it all in your life, you just need to find a healthy balance!

Starting my business was a very exciting time for me; it was new, it was a challenge, and it was my passion. I loved it so much, I felt like doing it all the time; it was all I thought about. What I didn't realize was that my relationship was deteriorating. I wasn't taking care of my body; I would get so involved with editing a video that, before I knew it, it was 2 a.m., and I hadn't gotten up to stretch once, and my neck and back were aching.

Once I was making money, I tried to make up for my neglect by turning my focus on improving my relationship and my health. I went to seminars and tried to discover what was holding me back in my relationship. I pulled all of my focus from my business and put it into my relationship. After a while, my business started to drop. I needed to find a healthy balance! Now, I set health goals, business goals, and book romantic dates. I think of ways to incorporate time with my family while I'm traveling on business, I take them with me, or I stop and visit them along the way. I linked my highest values together. YOU CAN HAVE IT ALL. Just balance it!

LINK YOUR HIGHEST VALUES!

There's only so much time in a day, and I knew I couldn't possibly do everything I desired. So, I started multitasking and did two things at once. I learned and educated myself while I exercised. I started to hike and listen to audio books. For a year straight, I hiked Diamond Head every morning and listened to Napoleon Hill's *Think and Grow Rich* and *Outwitting the Devil* by Sharon Lechter over and over. This was programming my mind, and the concepts became automatic for me. Instead of filling my mind with negative thoughts, I placed in positive ones. I was becoming more efficient.

I had business meetings while surfing, or I visited with people in my hot tub, because I needed to relax my body. When I said hot tub, people loved it! I love chatting and connecting with my friends, and I could do sit-ups while chatting! Instead of sitting in a meeting at the coffee shop, I could go for walks! People always ask me how I am able to get so much done. This is it: multitask and link your priorities! It will free up your time for other things.

IF YOU DON'T LIKE TO DO SOMETHING, LINK IT TO YOUR HIGHEST VALUE!

I learned this one from Dr. Demartini. When I started traveling for work, going from city to city, it was very exciting. After a while, the novelty wore off and I really didn't look forward to sitting on a plane for 11 hours! I was flying somewhere every month and sometimes twice a month; I spent a lot of hours on an airplane.

I chose to look at my travel differently, and what I saw was opportunity! I started planning things to get done on the plane. I love my business, so I would devote airplane time to working on my business plan, and I'd plan out my next three months. While I was writing this book, I looked forward to the plane rides. It gave me dedicated time to write, and the time went by really fast. Find what you like the most and then do it during the time you have to spend waiting or traveling.

RELATIONSHIPS.

YOU CAN'T GIVE WHAT YOU DON'T HAVE! Unless you feel trust in yourself, you can't trust others; if you don't accept yourself, you can't accept others. When people judge others, they are judging themselves the hardest. Once I stopped judging myself and started accepting myself for who I am, I was able to see and express that outwardly. I started accepting others, all the good and all the bad parts. I trusted myself, and it made it easier to trust others.

In my marriage, our relationship is strong because we both practice awareness, and we both see the value of personal growth. We have an understanding with each other; we are together because we desire and choose to be, not because we need each other. If I'm not happy in my relationship, it's because of something I'm feeling internally, and it's something I don't love about myself. My feelings are projected outwards. If I'm not feeling good enough inside, no matter what my husband does, it won't be enough.

Whenever I feel like I want to change or fix something about my husband, I know it's a sign to me that there's something inside I should love or release. I know that life is going to be challenging with anyone, so I have chosen to be with someone with whom, no matter what, I work out our issues, and we grow together. He inspires me to be a better person!

When you have a business, it helps to have peace and love in your relationships. When there's conflict or an unresolved issue, your mind and energy will go towards it. It will take up space in your mind and distract you from your dream.

I think of ways to include my family when I do business. We turn business trips into vacations for the whole family. It's nice to have the people I love there to experience the passion and inspiration I feel when I am chasing my passion.

My husband is so supportive of me, and he takes good care of me, making sure I eat healthy and take care of myself.

We are a great team. He reminds me to take breaks and rest. When I'm feeling scared or doubtful, he is my biggest cheerleader. He's got my back no matter what, and that kind of support brings tears to my eyes. When I think I can't do it, he believes in me.

When I was feeling fearful about how we were going to pay our bills, he said, "We will find a way. I know you; when you put your mind to it, you always manifest what your heart wants." One time I said, "Why aren't you stressed? Aren't you worried that we may lose our house if we can't make the mortgage payments?" He said, "I'm not stressed because I believe in you, I know you." I appreciate that he trusts me and believes in me more than I believe in myself sometimes.

If he had the same fears, he would be saying, "You're right; you'd better get a job, what if we go bankrupt?" That would increase my fear! Instead, he shows how he feels inside because he's at peace and not fearful. Behind this successful woman, there's a man who is like a solid and unmovable rock, and he lifts me and empowers me to be the woman I am!

My husband had his son when he was seventeen, and he had to work two jobs while struggling to pay the bills. When Ethan was five, he was in the military and he didn't get to spend much time with him while he was growing up. When we start our family, he wants to be the stay-at-home father. That fits so well with my vision because I desire to continue to invent products and empower the world, and I desire a family. This way, he can take more of the responsibility for taking care of the family. We both get to do what we love and we are contributing in different ways. Do what works for you, regardless of the opinions and judgments of others.

Most people see money as being the only source of a husband's contribution to a household. Even I had some conditioning around this, and it was something I had to work through. I attended Dr. Demartini's Master Planning seminar. We spent three days answering questions in his manual. This man is brilliant. He asks the right questions and it changed my perspective about my husband's contributions. I wrote down all the ways my husband contributes, and if I had to put a price on it, how much would it be worth to me. From the outside, people see that I'm working hard, making the money. But they don't see my husband's role behind the scenes.

EXERCISE:
SIGNIFICANT OTHER CONTRIBUTION

Try this if you don't feel grateful for your significant other:

1. Write down all the ways he/she contributes and put a price on it. It will immediately transform how you feel, and you will feel gratitude. It's a practice. So whenever you're feeling like you should look for a new partner, do this exercise. My husband's support is worth so much to me, I would rather he not work and support me than have a full-time job just to pay the bills. With him here supporting me, it allows me to make more and create more. And we can be together and have the freedom to travel and do whatever we desire when we desire. We can have lunch together or we can work out together. I'm fortunate that he has no problem with me being successful; while some men are intimidated by successful women, my man is bragging about me!

2. Write down all the ways your significant other supports you in your dreams. For example, my husband is an amazing cook. His cooking allows me to focus on my dreams. He takes Ethan to school, he fixes the house, etc. You will feel more gratitude if you focus your attention on what's great, instead of what's wrong. I see a balance, and we both feel we are fortunate to have each other. People say when they have a business, they don't have time for a relationship. But there are always solutions! YOU CAN HAVE IT ALL!

Thanks to my coaches, Kimber Kabell and David Blythe, I developed a practice scheduling activities weeks in advance. I sent in my weekly intentions and by the end of that week, I had to share the things

I completed (or didn't complete) as well as any challenges or wins I experienced. Doing this made it easy to be clear and focused for the week.

David had me scheduling my week so that each hour of the day was scheduled. I love it! I don't even have to think about what I'm going to do next; I already know. This is a great way to stay on track, there's no room for my conditioning to talk me out of it.

When I plan ahead, it's easy to create balance among my priorities. I desire to create balance; I desire it all! I schedule time in the morning to spend with Ethan, making breakfast before he goes to school, and I schedule work. When you work from home, it's easier to be interrupted. When I schedule work time, everyone in the family respects the time and supports my commitments.

Also, everyone feels loved and important because there is enough time and energy being shared equally. When Ethan looked at my schedule, and saw "Ethan time, movie night," he was excited. You can make time for everything. I schedule breaks, meals, and workouts. I make sure that, each day, I make time for physical activity. After a good morning surf, I come back recharged and inspired. Often, I think of solutions while I'm surfing, so it's important that I do make the time! I am aligning my passions.

EXERCISE:

I am including a sample scheduling chart that you can use. Try it for a week and see how you feel. Try it for 90 days, and create new behavior!

WEEKLY SCHEDULE CHART
Planner for Weekly Goals

The Week of : _____

DATE							
	Sunday	Monday	Tuesday	Wednesday	Thursday	Friday	Saturday
8:00							
8:30							
9:00							
9:30							
10:00							
10:30							
11:00							
11:30							
12:00							
12:30							
1:00							
1:30							
2:00							
2:30							
3:00							
3:30							
4:00							
4:30							
5:00							
5:30							
6:00							
6:30							
7:00							
7:30							
8:00							
8:30							

NO WORK

	MON	TUE	WED	THURS	FRI	SAT	SUN
	6:00 Emails	MEDITATION SIT	EMAILL	MEDITATION SIT	SIT	SIT	MEDITATION SIT
	SIT	MAI TIME SURF	SIT	MAI TIME SURF or Snorkel	EMAILS	WALK	SIT WALK
	ETHAN JASON		ETHAN JASON Farmers Market		WAIPO Vally Hike	JASON FAMILY DAY	JASON
	WORK	WORK	WORK				
	LUNCH 1-1:30	LUNCH	LUNCH	LUNCH	LUNCH	LUNCH	LUNCH FREE DAY
	WORK	WORK	WORK	WORK JASON WD		FAMILY DAY	
	BOXING	BOXING	BOXING				
	DINNER	DINNER	DINNER	DINNER	DINNER DATE NIGHT JASON	DINNER	DINNER
		ETHAN MOVIE	ART				
	BOOK	BOOK	BOOK	BOOK	BOOK	BOOK	BOOK

Mai's Schedule Chart

Be sure and book time for yourself. It's important to have time to take care of you, and have some alone time and independence. My husband and I both work at home, so we're together a lot. It's not a problem, I love being with him. However, when I go surfing or travel for business, it's nice because we miss each other. We appreciate each other more. As the saying goes, "Absence makes the heart grow fonder."

I love doing things for others, but it's nice to do something that I desire for me. If it's time to just go for a walk, get a pedicure or massage, or hang out on the beach, schedule that in, or your life will get too busy.

When I set commitments and then follow through on them, it builds my trust and confidence. I stay on purpose and it makes it clear to see the next step. I was applying scheduling to my life in business and at home, so I thought I would try applying to my diet.

While training for the fitness challenge, I created a schedule detailing what I could eat and at what time. It made it easy to stay committed.

When you schedule your life around your desires, you will get much more done. I get excited when I add things I desire to my schedule; I know it will get done!

On the opposite page is an example of one of my charts. I made sure I added both business and personal time. It's useful to color code. Life happens, so I do give myself some flexibility and I update it every month.

CHILDHOOD!

I feel so fortunate to have entrepreneurial parents. From a young age, I watched my parents grow, from being poor and having nothing, into successful, wealthy retirees. They taught me how to work hard, do my best, keep my word, and follow through.

Children learn more from what their parents do than from what they say. I learned from their actions and behaviors. They didn't have to tell me anything; I learned by observing. I watched as my mom found solutions to every challenge. I watched her take risks and adapt to change.

I used to regret that my mom hadn't taught me how to play volleyball or martial arts when I was a child. Starting that young would have given me a real advantage! What I realize now is that my mom started training me at a young age to become an entrepreneur instead.

My parents showed me that it was possible to improve, and you had to be flexible. When my parents clothing manufacture sales started to go down, they saw that embroidery was popular, so they invested in an embroidery machine and added embroidery to their services. Their sales went up! When the embroidery sales went down, they bought a restaurant, and the restaurant income balanced everything out! I applied that concept when I was hairstyling. Hair extensions were popular, so I invested in further training so I could provide extensions to my customers. I had recently started a new job, and I was becoming a specialist. I automatically increased my income. Even local celebrities were requesting my services because I was one of the few who knew how to do it. And, of course, I was very good at it!

BE THE BEST IN YOUR INDUSTRY
AND ALWAYS LEARN AND SPECIALIZE IN YOUR FIELD.

CHILDREN!

My stepson is also learning by watching me and imitating my behaviors. When I was developing my brand for speaking events, I created a logo with my name; "M.A.I – Manifest-Achieve-Inspire." My stepson said, "Mom, you know how you did MAI? I did one for me: ETHAN-Energetic-Thoughtful-Helpful-Annoying-Noisy." It was so cute. I said, "Good for you; those are the words you think you are. Now, let's do one with words that you desire to become!" He was really excited, and he came up with Enthusiastic-Tough-Hardworking-Active-Neat. I didn't even tell him to do the first one; he was just inspired to do it for himself!

When I see him mirroring my actions, it gives me relief. I thought I would have to tell him how to do things, and I didn't know how I was going to do that! I've discovered that it's actually pretty simple; I get to just be me, and he learns from it. I always try to practice what I preach. If I tell him not to do something, but then I go and do it, he picks up on it and calls me on it, "But you do it." Never underestimate the power of learning through experience.

After a few weeks at a new school, Ethan came home very upset and said, "I don't want go back to school; I want you to home school me." I asked, "What happened?" He said, "I bumped into this guy by accident, and he was upset and started to bully me." I told him, "You know, bullying happens everywhere, not just in school. When I go surfing, some girls bully me, but when I stand up for myself, they back off. Bullying will happen outside of school. What will you do then? Just because you were bullied, doesn't mean you can quit school."

I continued, "You may seem like an easy target, so they bully you. Let's build you so you are tough, and can stand up for yourself. I'll teach you some kung fu!"

When I learned kung fu at 19, I felt so empowered. I knew that in any situation, I could take care of myself, even against men. They wouldn't be expecting a side kick to the head from a little girl. It felt good to know how to defend myself.

So, I taught Ethan a few moves, including my award-winning block-punch! After a few weeks of training, he said he felt confident that if anything happened, he could take care of himself. His increase in self-confidence must have shown on the outside because the boy stopped picking on him, apologized, and now they're friends!

Seven months later, Ethan came home frustrated and said, "Mom I don't like my school; they're teaching me things that I learned two years ago, plus kids are always interrupting. We can never move along in class. I want to go to another one." I said, "Okay, if that's what you want. You may have to sit on the bus for two hours a day because the next school is an hour away. We could try challenging you with some extra online courses so you are learning more, or if the schools here aren't good enough, you could go back to Georgia to finish school."

He was only seeing the drawbacks of the school. I helped him realize that there were also drawbacks to not going to that school and that the grass isn't always greener on the other side.

He sat with it for a while. The next day, I said, "You know, Ethan, we can homeschool you if it isn't working out." He said, "It's okay, Mom; it's just that kids naturally don't like to go to school. It's not the school; it's really not that bad. I guess I was feeling like I didn't fit because I'm one of the few Haole's in the class." (Haole is a Hawaiian word referring to individuals of *White* ancestry.) I said, "You know, I was the only Asian person in my class when I went to school in Canada. I actually felt special! I bet all the girls like you." He said, "You're right, the girls do like me. They say they like my country accent!"

I showed him the benefits of being the only White person and he became positive about going back to school. I just helped him see both sides: the good and the bad. Sometimes, when you think things are bad, it's because you don't see the other side of the situation. You are only focusing on the negative. If you see the benefits, it won't seem bad anymore.

I enrolled Ethan in a kids' leadership workshop and it brought us all closer as a family. After the workshop, he told me he already knew a lot of the stuff because we'd taught him. It's so inspiring to hear that by practicing my own awareness and growth, it was rubbing off on our son.

When you live your life with fulfillment and happiness, that happiness overflows all around you, and influences your children and others around you. It starts from within. Look inside you and see what you can draw out that brings you passion. What is your dream?

SHOWING APPRECIATION.

When I started to set goals for my business, I also set a goal to create a better relationship with my family. My parents showed me that family was important, and something to be valued and treasured. We already had a great relationship; there was nothing we wouldn't do for each other. My parents worked hard to provide for the family. Growing up, my Dad worked two businesses and didn't take any vacation or holidays, no days off at all, not even weekends, and he worked from 7:30 a.m. to 1 a.m. My mom was running the clothing manufacturing business, and she worked hard too! I was grateful to have such loving parents. Perhaps it was a cultural thing, but we never grew up saying the words "I love you" or hugging each other.

I desired to tell my parents how much I loved them and how much I appreciated them. So one night, I called up my dad and said, "Hey, Dad, what are you doing?" He was watching TV. I said, "I just wanted to say I really appreciate you working so hard to provide for us…" My voice started to crack up and I started to cry, but I told him I loved him. I said what I had to say. When I was finished, there was an awkward silence, so I said, "Okay, bye."

The next day, my older brother Mau called me and said, "Hey, so Dad said you had a bad dream and called?" It was so funny! I told my brother what really happened, and he was inspired to do the same. He was braver than me; he did it in person. He told me he went while my dad was working at the warehouse, and when he tried to hug him, my dad went into a martial arts stance to block him. It was by reflex. Mau said it was really awkward! That story still makes us both laugh!

Both my brothers were inspired to take the PSI seminar after I took mine. I told them it was great, and they trusted me. Both my brothers loved it, and they got so much out of it. All three of us set goals to say "I love you" to our parents. The only one left was my younger brother, Sing. When Sing told my dad he loved him, my dad said, "Sing, are you okay? What happened? Did something bad happen?" He was so worried; he thought he had gotten into trouble. It was not the norm in our family, so when we did it, he thought that there must have been something wrong. Thinking about these things always puts a smile on my face.

Dropping an "I love you" had been a big risk for all of us. Sing took it one step further and set a goal for his ninety-day program to say, "I love you" to my parents every day. IT TAKES NINETY DAYS TO CREATE A NEW BEHAVIOR. Taking that next step made it easier for all of us to say it. Now my mom says it all the time!

I encourage you to do the same. If you haven't told your family how much you care about them, do it now before it's too late.

WHEN YOU SHOW APPRECIATION IN ANY RELATIONSHIP, IT GROWS.

Who haven't you talked to in a long time? Call them up. If you have any resentment, clear it up. It's not worth holding onto any grudge. It just drains you and blocks you from being inspired. You can't be inspired when you are feeling anger or resentment.

Our relationship with our parents kept getting better. You don't have to have a bad relationship to take steps to make it better. We were great as a family, but now our love is even deeper. My parents are getting old, so I desire to say "I love you" as often as I can, and show them how much I appreciate them. They did everything for our family, and I desire to take care of them now that I can.

That year, my younger brother made it a goal to take his siblings on a vacation, just the three of us. He let me decide, so I picked Australia. Life gets busy, so I was so grateful to have taken the time to experience this family trip together. My family is the biggest support I have, and they have been and always will be there for me.

When I was traveling in Europe, studying hair, I managed to max out my credit card, and my younger brother paid it off for me. We have a great relationship; we communicate well with each other, and we share our deepest secrets. They come to me with their challenges, and vice versa. When I started my business, they supported me from the beginning.

My parents started to wonder why we shared our appreciation so much after completing the PSI seminars. They didn't know what it was about, but they loved the growth and transformation they were seeing in their children. Eight years after I took the class, my parents enrolled! I got them a Chinese translator, and they finally understood why I was so passionate about awareness practice and self-development.

VOLUNTEER AND GIVE BACK!

I always make time to help my community and give back. I've volunteered at the Hawaii Women and Children's Shelter, giving them new haircuts with the CreaClip! I've also volunteered at the women's prison. I was invited to give an inspirational speech for the girls at a private school in Hawaii to inspire and teach them about the inventing process.

It was so special for me to speak to those twelve- and thirteen-year-old girls. When I was their age, I had great ideas for inventions. But because I was only twelve, I didn't know what the next step was, and I didn't have any guidance.

I desired to help these girls, and they were so engaged! One girl kept asking if she could be my CreaNails model. Two other girls asked if they could have their hair cut with the CreaClip. The girls were so excited about the product, we had to stop them from cutting their own hair! They couldn't wait to try it on themselves, and on each other. We only had time to cut three models.

Wouldn't it be neat if one of the girls in that workshop followed through and invented a product?

When I was young, I used to pretend I was a teacher in front of a class, and here I was, years later, in front of the class with girls eager to learn. You never know what's possible until you take the next step!

Putting on an invention workshop for the girls at a private school.
Inspiring them to follow their dreams!

I know this is just the beginning; there are so many ways I can contribute. My vision is to have my own foundation so I can mentor and give scholarships to young entrepreneurs to support them in following their dreams.

Everyone has great ideas, they just don't know what the next step is.

HOW YOU DO ONE THING IS HOW YOU DO EVERYTHING!

I am a perfectionist in everything that I do. And it's high on my values. When I did martial arts, I desired to be perfect. It was the same with being a hairstylist; each cut had to be perfect. When I danced, I practiced and practiced until I reached perfection in my mind. When I created success in one area, it was easy for me to create success in another area.

My cousin said, "Mai, I call you gold fingers because everything you touch turns to gold." When I look back, I can see that it was just my thought processes: never give up, always do your best, persist, follow through, and always, always, always take the next step. Using these thought processes, I am able to duplicate success; I can turn things into gold. So can you. Take a look at the thought processes that are helping or hindering you. When you are aware of them, it gives you an opportunity to choose something different, to create a different result!

YOUR THINKING AFFECTS HOW YOU SEE AND DO EVERYTHING. ENJOY THE JOURNEY!

It's never about the goal; it's about the journey. Reaching a goal is not what's important. Look at how you reached the goal. If you got there by neglecting your body or did it for the wrong reasons, reaching the goal is not as fulfilling. My journey to success has been powerful, and I have loved every step of it.

Take time to pause and appreciate every lesson, and appreciate the growth. Pause to celebrate the little wins. My ego voice said, "You have to make a million dollars; then you will be successful." I had to accept myself as successful now; otherwise, when I achieved my goal and made the million dollars, my ego would say, "It's not enough. You need to make five million dollars; then you will be successful."

Other people thought I was successful, but I didn't believe I was until I made a million. I thought, WHAT IS IT THAT OTHER PEOPLE SEE THAT I DON'T? If more than three people say the same thing to me, I start taking it seriously.

I spent a whole year just owning my success, and I acknowledged myself as being successful. As soon as I changed my thinking, the money rolled in, and I started to create millions.

WHEN YOU REALIZE THAT NOTHING IS MISSING, WHAT YOU ARE SEEKING WILL COME!

RESULTS!

I heard this from a PSI seminar: "The ultimate judge is results. Sometimes harsh, always fair! " I always look at my results, and it shows what my thinking is. If I'm real honest with myself, I admit what works and doesn't work in my life. My results show what I have learned and what I am practicing. The concepts are in my head, and my results are proof that they are working!

You may talk the talk, but you also have to walk the walk. You cannot say that you know how to reduce stress, when in actuality you are completely stressed out. You also cannot say your relationship is extremely important when all you really focus on is your career.

DO YOU KNOW IT, OR DO YOU KNOW ABOUT IT?

Your results and life will show what you practice. Use this to your advantage and see where you are struggling. Assess where you can shift and grow. Unless a person has already done something, don't take advice from them. People would give me all kinds of advice and it would influence me, even though they had no idea about my industry. My mentor said, "If they haven't licensed a product, maybe you shouldn't ask them for advice."

It made sense.

ASK ADVICE FROM PEOPLE WHO HAVE ALREADY DONE OR ARE PRACTICING WHAT YOU ARE SEEKING!

WHAT SET OF GLASSES ARE YOU WEARING? Are they rose-colored glasses or dark glasses? Are they clean and bright and clear? If they are dark, you won't be able to see everything you need to see. If we always focus on things that are wrong, the whole world starts to look wrong.

EXERCISE:

CHANGING NEGATIVE THOUGHT PATTERNS

Each time you have a negative thought, write it down. You will become aware of the times you are thinking negatively. When you are not aware, it's hard to make a change. Each time you notice a negative thought, make a conscious shift and direct your thought in a more positive direction. The more times you do this, the sooner you will create a new behavior. Tally each time you do this in a day and reward yourself when you experience improvement. Build that positivity muscle!

GO FOR IT!

Stop holding back and just go for it! The universe gave you an idea because you were ready for it. Trust that everything happens for a reason, and that it is the right time to follow your dreams. You are reading this book because you are seeking. When you commit, the universe will provide you with everything. Trust, take one action step and then the next, and never give up! The life of your dreams is ahead. Follow your dreams; GO FOR IT! You can make your dreams a reality!

ACKNOWLEDGEMENTS

I would like to acknowledge my parents, Kim and Vinh Lieu; they have been great role models and an inspiration to me. I couldn't have done it without the love and support of family: my brothers Sing and Mau Lieu and sister-in-law Sabrina Lee Lieu. My husband, Jason Dunn, for always believing in me. You are the biggest cheerleader, and I love you. My stepson Ethan and in-laws for inspiring me to grow. My sponsors Victor and Elfriede Fisher, Elizabeth Walker, and the Ring family that brought my family to Canada to have the opportunity to create a life without limits. My life coach, David Blythe, for your willingness to guide me in my awareness practice. My business coach, Kimber Kabell, for seeing me bigger than I see myself. Coach Haaheo for endless support. Howard Lim for your expertise and treating me like your little sister. Tony Ly for your creativity. Sifu Alex Kwok for bringing so many new experiences in my life. Thank you to my Math teacher, Mr. Martin, for instilling positive thoughts in me at a young age. Thank you to PSI seminars, Living Compassion, Breakthrough Experience, Ike Pono Quest, CEOSpace, BrainStorm, and mentors Cheri Huber, Dr. Demartini, Marshall Thurber, Michael Beckwith, Bob Proctor, Sharon Lechter, Lisa Nichols, BJ Dorhmann, Mark Victor Hansen, Bob Circosta, and Tom Wilhite for all the new awareness and growth I've experience throughout my journey; you all are an inspiration to me. Also, special thanks to all my friends and fans on Facebook and YouTube, I love you all.

TAKE THE NEXT STEP

TAKE THE NEXT STEP

_____

_____

_____

_____

_____

_____

_____

_____

_____

_____

_____

_____

_____

_____

_____

_____

_____

_____

_____

_____

_____

_____

TAKE THE NEXT STEP

_____

_____

_____

_____

_____

_____

_____

_____

_____

_____

_____

_____

_____

_____

_____

_____

_____

_____

_____

_____

TAKE THE NEXT STEP

TAKE THE NEXT STEP

Proudly Published by

Be Inspired. Be Motivated. Be Entertained.

www.bethatbooks.com

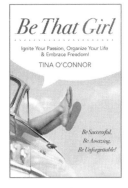

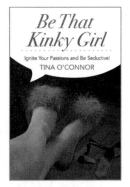

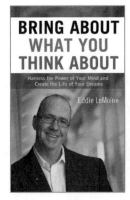

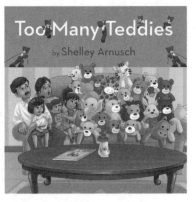